Communication Skills Training

How to Talk to Anyone about Anything and Immediately Improve Your Social Intelligence, Active Listening Skills, and Public Speaking

Free Bonus from Andy Gardner

Hi!

My name is Andy Gardner, and first off, I want to THANK YOU for reading my book.

Now you have a chance to join my exclusive email list related to human psychology and self-development so you can get the ebook below for free as well as the potential to get more ebooks for free! Simply click the link below to join.

P.S. Remember that it's 100% free to join the list.

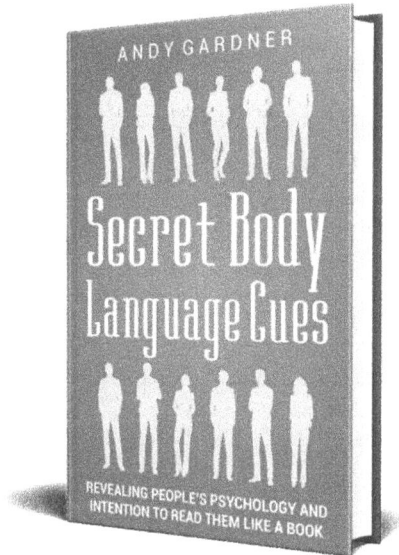

Access your free bonuses here:
https://livetolearn.lpages.co/communication-skills-training-paperback/

Table of Contents

Introduction

What if we all had the same speaking tones, body language, and facial expressions? Imagine that nothing in how we speak changed, regardless of the situation or message we're trying to deliver. It would be tough to understand what anyone was trying to say, right?

A simple phrase, such as "Well done!" can be used in either a cheerful or sarcastic context. "That's it!" can either mean "stop" or "Yes, what you're doing is right! Keep it up." Putting something into words is not enough. You can never know what a person truly means if they don't try to communicate it to you. Communication is a two-way street. Communication skills are a person's ability to deliver a message effectively via numerous tools, including tone, context, body language, facial expression, active listening, and being straightforward.

Being a great communicator is an indispensable life skill. It is crucial to the success of your career, achieving your personal goals, and maintaining healthy relationships. While some people are born communicators, others struggle to communicate their messages, get tongue-tied, and mumble. The good news is that you can learn and develop the ability to communicate effectively, just like any other skill.

We don't only use our communication skills when we need to convey an idea or express our feelings. These skills are also used whenever we receive any kind of information. This is because a large part of our communication skills depends on our ability to listen, observe, process, empathize, and react. Excellent communicators are aware of other people's styles of interaction through observing communication on different mediums, understanding that those styles vary depending on the place, environment, and means of interaction. Some people express their emotions more effectively through phone conversations than physical interactions. Other people are better at communicating via text, although this form of communication is always subject to misunderstandings. You may find it hard to speak your mind in public, but you easily share your ideas in private spaces.

Excellent communication skills guarantee that everyone will understand you and that you understand them too. Good communicators are generally self-assured and confident. Not worrying about misinterpreted conversations takes a significant load off your shoulders.

Reading this book will give you a greater understanding of why communication skills are highly valued, especially in today's world. You'll learn about the different skills and their characteristics, how to be an active listener, and how to hear the emotions behind people's words. You'll learn how mastering body language is the key to maintaining an engaging conversation.

The best thing about this book is that it offers practical information on how to start a conversation with anyone, even if you're an introvert. It offers numerous strategies to help you initiate conversations with others while leaving great first impressions. You'll also learn how to master the art of storytelling, so you can keep people interested and engaged. Then, you'll come across step-by-step instructions showing you how to manage arguments and end conversations without feeling awkward.

Chapter 1: The Why behind Communication Skills

In this chapter, you'll learn everything you need to know about why you need to develop your communication skills. You'll learn the benefits of being a good communicator and understand the different types of communication you can use. Finally, you'll read about the different styles and how they can be used daily.

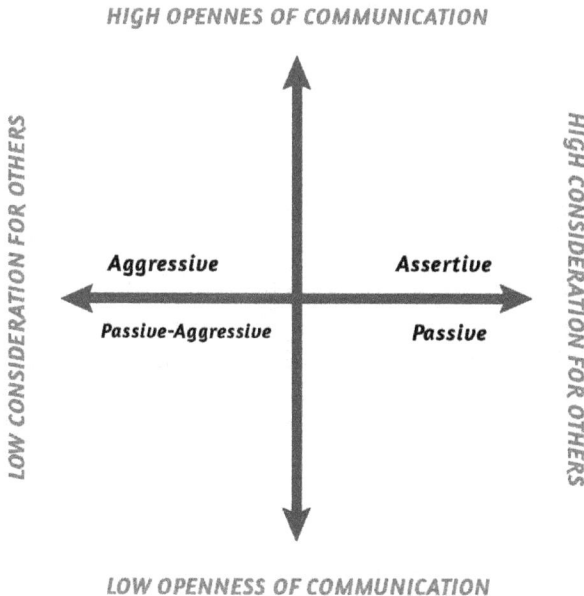

HIGH OPENNES OF COMMUNICATION

LOW CONSIDERATION FOR OTHERS

HIGH CONSIDERATION FOR OTHERS

Aggressive   Assertive

Passive-Aggressive   Passive

LOW OPENNESS OF COMMUNICATION

The Benefits of Having Excellent Communication Skills

Having good communication skills is an invaluable asset in both personal and professional settings. The ability to be understood and understand others depends on cultivating mutual trust and respect, which are essentially the foundation of all healthy relationships. Communicating effectively with others helps you build up and maintain strong relationships. Lacking this skill can drive a wedge between you and those around you. Speaking your mind and expressing yourself eloquently allows you to cultivate and maintain good social, romantic, familial, and professional relationships.

People with excellent communication skills are generally more confident and assured. If you're worried about not getting your message through to your audience, you could be seen as hesitant and full of self-doubt. This is a compelling reason people with great communication skills receive more job offers than the average person. They never sell themselves short! Since most disagreements arise from misunderstandings or refusal to tolerate an opposing point of view, excellent communicators are rarely subject to conflict.

Great ideas mean nothing if they are not appropriately communicated. Imagine how many great inventions never made it because their creators were inarticulate and failed to pitch them compellingly.

The benefits of having good communication skills are countless. Here are a few things that being a good communicator can do for you:

Creates a Healthy Work Environment

You can create a healthy work environment for yourself and others by learning to communicate effectively. Trust is the most critical factor in positive workplaces. Coworkers who don't trust each other won't work well together and will always be in competition. While some competition is needed to maintain a productive and exciting work environment, too much competition can lead to discord, a lack of unity, and unhappy organization-client relationships. This is because employees start prioritizing personal goals and lose sight of the bigger picture.

When you nurture a sense of trust between you and your coworkers, you'll be able to promote positive attitudes and stronger relationships. This can relieve some of the tension and stress which occurs in the workplace, which can reduce misunderstandings.

Helps You Succeed in Your Career Path

Excellent communication skills can help you succeed in your career path, regardless of your industry. Whether you communicate directly with clients, report to your manager, participate in group projects or oversee a team, your success largely depends on your ability to communicate effectively. While each job comes with different structures, challenges, and communication dynamics, the skills you need to excel in this area are universal.

It helps to observe how everyone around you interacts so you can start mimicking and building on these insights. Not only will this help you develop your skills, but it also allows you to understand others which can help you diffuse conflicts and become a better negotiator.

Makes You Appear Charismatic and Attractive

There's a thin line between knowing how to communicate and being an effective communicator. Like all other skills, you must continue nurturing and developing your communication skills. If you don't continue learning, you'll lose your capacity to communicate your message effectively.

How you communicate with others is an entire process that begins the moment you enter the room. How you carry and present yourself and the first impression you make all count toward your communication skill set. Imagine you're a salesman meeting up with a client to sell them a luxurious watch. How will your client respond to your effort? Even if you build up an extraordinary pitch, if you walk in with a slouchy posture in sweatpants and start stumbling over your words, your communication will be less effective. They'll likely turn down your offer. Your appearance and attitude play a part in your overall message.

How you look and behave must be relevant to whatever you're trying to communicate. You should also be able to appeal to the person you're dealing with and capture their imagination. We often forget that most of our conversations are about the people we're talking to and not about ourselves. Even if you're recounting a particular event in your life, your sentence structure, vocabulary, and what you choose to tell or leave out all depend on who you're talking to. Try to figure out as much as you can about the person's personality, beliefs, and interests so you can appeal to them and address them appropriately. Learn to respect other people's opinions even when they don't align with your own, and practice active listening. This makes it easier to get along with others.

Improves Your Problem-Solving Skills

Having good problem-solving skills enriches your personal and professional life. If you're filling a managerial position, you probably already know this skill is essential if you are a team leader or manager. It also makes you more adaptable to change and allows you to quickly deal with conflicts. Problem-solvers can handle unexpected situations without being held back by fear and anxiety. Those with good communication skills are active listeners and can empathize with others. They know which questions to ask to find the answers they're searching for. Good communicators can tell when they can step in to help someone or listen to them and when to let them sort things out independently. They know exactly what to say to people whenever they're struggling.

Allows You to Feel Better about Yourself

How you communicate with others determines how much you can connect with them. You can't get to know someone intimately if you don't know how to communicate well with them. Being an excellent communicator requires you to be an honest and authentic speaker. Communicating in a genuine way that aligns with who you truly are will make you feel good about yourself.

Offers a Sense of Direction and Clarity

People only know what to expect of you, whether at work or in your personal life, if you can communicate your plans, objectives, and wishes to them. They also know what you expect of them in a friendship, romantic relationship, or as a team member at work. This sense of clarity is critical at work because it helps you and your team identify problems whenever something isn't heading in the right direction. Developing communication skills also teaches you to effectively deliver constructive feedback, which is needed to steer things onto the right track. Setting clear expectations for those in your life can help you maintain healthy relationships, ensure no one crosses your boundaries, and avoid conflicts. It enables you to determine when your efforts aren't being reciprocated and allows you to communicate exactly how you feel.

Fosters Better Relationships

Communication is vital when it comes to any relationship. Communicating your interests, thoughts, needs, desires, feelings, and emotions and actively listening to those of others is essential to the maintenance of healthy relationships. You must also be able to speak up if they hurt you so that you can work together toward a resolution. Some people prefer to let hurtful situations slide. However, they don't realize that they're slowly accumulating all their friend's or partners' faults, which eventually leads to resentment. It's essential to be able to talk about anything with those who are closest to you. Otherwise, undesirable feelings, which will ultimately ruin the relationship, will arise.

Keeps You Engaged

Good communication skills come with better comprehension and confidence. When you know exactly what you need to do and grow confident in your abilities, you become more engaged at work and in your passions and hobbies. If you're a manager, communicating with your employees can increase their job satisfaction and make them feel more engaged.

Enhances Productivity

Communicating with your employees or coworkers lets you understand each other's roles and expectations. When everything is clearly communicated from the beginning, everyone can focus on doing their work instead of wasting time on things that don't matter. This applies to every part of life. For instance, talking to your partner about your plans and to-do list, and asking them to wash the dishes, instead of waiting for you to come back home would be a lot more effective than complaining about having so much on your plate and expecting them to help out on their own initiative. The latter situation would result in an easily avoidable argument and leave you with additional chores.

How Effective Communication Changed Ian's Life

This is what Ian told us about his life:

"I wasn't always great at communicating with others, particularly when it came to my needs, expectations, and feelings. I expected everyone to know what I expected from them without uttering a single word about it. I expected them to know how to deal with me when I was feeling down, when to leave me alone, and when to try to get me to talk. I thought they already knew how I like to be joked around with - what was acceptable for me and what wasn't. I expected everyone to stick to their boundaries and mine, even though I'd never communicated them.

Guess what I did when my expectations weren't met. I felt uncomfortable with someone's jokes or banter, or when someone crossed my boundaries. I gave them the cold shoulder until I felt like talking to them again. I didn't bother to explain why I distanced myself from anyone, which left them confused. The more someone repeated their "mistakes" (or actions that they had no idea bothered me at all), the colder and more distant I grew. This sounds very toxic, doesn't it?

I knew that the way I was behaving was wrong, but I didn't have the energy or the know-how to remedy the situation. It was easier to let people go or figure things out on their own than to try to communicate with them. It wasn't until I started to lose people who meant the world to me that I realized that I had to do something.

This is when I decided to learn how to start communicating. In the beginning, it was very hard for me to start telling people that they hurt me when they did this or that or that it bothered me when someone joked about one of my insecurities. I worried that I'd come off as uptight if I listed my boundaries or said that I didn't like it when someone disrespected or made fun of me, even as a joke. However, I knew that it was unfair to everyone around me.

Communicating with others didn't make me appear vulnerable or defensive like I thought it would. If anything, people started trusting and respecting me more. They no longer walked on eggshells around me, and I noticed that my relationships grew significantly stronger. I no longer felt horrible for treating my loved ones the way I did. I never admitted the fact that I knew that they deserved better."

Types of Communication

There are several types of communication. However, the following seven are the most popular ones:

Verbal Communication

Verbal communication is the chief method of communication. We all use it to communicate and deliver our messages to others.

Verbal communication is broken down into oral and written communication. Face-to-face or phone conversations are examples of the former, while a written letter or text message is an example of written communication.

Non-Verbal Communication

This is a subtler type of communication, and it encompasses any form of communication that is non-verbal and not written. This includes body language, posture, gestures, eye contact, and facial expressions. People underestimate the expressive effectiveness of being able to communicate without saying much. Most of our emotions are conveyed through this skill.

Watch any movie you've never seen before. Turn the volume and any subtitles off. You'll probably be able to tell whether the character is happy, sad, angry, neutral, or surprised just by observing their facial reactions, hand gestures, and body language.

Written Communication

Written communication is a subtype of verbal communication and refers to expressing oneself using written words. Blogs, articles, emails, text messages, and letters are all types of written communication.

Oral Communication

This is another subtype of verbal communication, and it refers to interacting via spoken word. TV reporters, talk shows, face-to-face conversations, speeches, seminars, lectures, and phone calls are all examples of oral communication. This is considered the best communication skill that anyone can master because you can tweak your language and tone of voice to deliver the desired emotion along with your message.

Active Listening

Many people don't know that active listening is a communication skill. It is one of the most important, for that matter. Active listening requires you to mindfully listen to others and take the time to process and reflect on their words. You must be attentive to the speaker's thoughts, emotions, and feelings.

Visual Communication

Visual communication refers to the expression of thoughts and feelings through visual media. The pictures you come across on blogs are examples of visual communication. Videos, stickers, and gifs are all examples of visual communication. Our activities on social media platforms like Instagram and Snapchat rely on this form of communication.

Mass Communication

This type of communication refers to sharing information with a large audience, such as via newspapers or TV. Like verbal communication, this skill comes in oral and written forms.

Communication Styles

There are four different communication styles - how people communicate, which is different for everyone. However, there are four main styles, and if you can identify them, you'll be able to navigate the minefield that mixed messages can leave in their wake, such as misunderstandings, misinterpretations, and arguments. Understanding the different communication styles can help you interact with different people more effectively.

Passive Communication Style

These types of communicators like to avoid the spotlight. They are generally quiet and are often indifferent during arguments and debates. They seldom take a stand or show any assertive behavior. Passive individuals don't talk about their feelings or needs, which is why you'll struggle to determine whether or not they're feeling uncomfortable or need guidance.

Here are some signs you're dealing with a passive communicator:

- They can't say "no."
- They have a soft voice
- They are generally apologetic
- They avoid making eye contact
- They're easy-going
- They have a poor posture
- They fidget often

When dealing with passive communicators, it's best to be straightforward and initiate private conversations. Ask for their input and opinions to make them feel involved, and avoid asking "yes" or "no" questions.

You must start developing your communication skills if you're a passive communicator. Seize the opportunity to speak up whenever you can do so comfortably. Experiment with written communications until you ease into oral ones.

Aggressive Communication Style

These communicators allow their thoughts and feelings to get in the way. They behave and speak impulsively without thinking about their actions all the way through. This compromises their social and professional relationships and decreases their productivity at work.

The following are some signs of aggressive communicators:

- They interrupt others while they're speaking
- They have an overbearing posture
- They maintain firm eye contact
- They usually invade other people's personal spaces

You need to approach an aggressive communicator calmly while maintaining your assertiveness. If they're your coworker, avoid discussing their feelings or personal issues by keeping the conversation strictly professional. You need to know when to walk away from this individual, so you don't risk wasting your time or getting into an argument.

If you're an aggressive communicator, you need to work on introducing positive communication techniques into your life. It will also help to reduce stress levels.

Passive-Aggressive Communication Style

Passive-aggressive communicators approach situations aggressively – especially people driven by passion and motivation while appearing passive on the outside. While so the language they use is calm and sweet, their actions are the complete opposite. These individuals are excellent manipulators- they steer everything in a direction that only benefits them.

Passive-aggressive individuals often:

- Behave sarcastically
- Exhibit denial tendencies
- Look happy even though they're feeling down
- Mutter
- Resort to the silent treatment

Make straightforward requests when dealing with this type of person, so you leave no room for confusion or debate. Always make sure you confront their unacceptable behavior. Get their honest opinion by asking for their feedback.

If you have this communication style, practice communicating your thoughts and feelings with others.

Assertive

This is the most productive communication style in the workplace. These people are respected among their colleagues and can share their ideas and thoughts openly and confidently with others. They have no problem taking on new challenges but are never afraid to say "no" or create strict boundaries.

Those individuals:

- Use frequent gestures
- Have great sharing abilities and collaboration skills
- Have a good posture
- Speak in a clear voice
- Are able to make friendly eye contact

- Express their thoughts and feelings effectively

When dealing with an assertive communicator, you should encourage them to speak up. If possible, give them leadership roles and ask them to help people with other communication styles. Work out what type of communicator you are from the information provided in this chapter. You can learn all about active listening in the following chapter. Active listening is among the most critical communication skills, which is why you'll benefit from learning how to improve on that front.

Chapter 2: How to Truly Listen

Do you ever feel like you're just sitting there, not contributing to a conversation you're listening to? You shouldn't feel uninvolved because communication requires both the speaker and the listener.

Communication requires both the speaker and the listener.
https://www.pexels.com/photo/photo-of-women-talking-to-each-other-4051134/

The speaker is the one who sends the message during communication, while the listener is the one who receives it. Communication breaks down if there is any break in the delivery by the speaker and the listener is confused or does not understand the message. There is a disconnect between the speaker and the listener.

This is about more than just hearing. It's also about comprehending what you hear, which tells you that the listener is just as important as the speaker. Effective listening is a necessary skill because it helps the listener understand and process the message being sent and, as a result, respond or act in the right way. This also helps the speaker.

So, we must learn how to truly listen. Does that sound strange? Even if it does, you should know that being silent during a conversation or a lecture does not really mean that you are paying attention.

You'll realize this when there's a small silence in the conversation, and you find yourself at a loss to describe what you've heard so far. If you're really listening, you'll instantly pick up on the main points of the message being conveyed and be able to rephrase it in your own words so that it keeps its authenticity and intention when it's conveyed to another listener.

If you can do this, it means you have listened to the message in its entirety without skimming, interrupting, or otherwise disrupting the speaker, and you understand what was being said.

If you want to be a good communicator, you must first learn to truly listen. In other words, before being a good communicator, you must first be an effective listener.

This will be covered in depth in the sections below.

What Is Effective Listening?

When you listen effectively, you pay attention to what is said, process the information correctly, and respond appropriately. As you can see, it goes beyond simply listening. Effective listening skills help boost your awareness, as well as your communication habits.

Importance of Effective Listening

As you learn to be a more effective listener, you'll find that your productivity and output grow. You'll be more in tune with the discussion and ready to tackle the challenge at hand. You can get the job done without making any mistakes or having to start again.

Listening also plays a large part in relationships. When people make concerted efforts to listen to one another, they develop better attitudes toward each other. This builds trust and a healthier relationship.

The following are the benefits of effective listening in everyday settings.

Effective Listening in Management and Supervision

The ability to listen attentively is crucial for any manager, whether they deal with human resources or oversee projects.

This ability helps you understand what your coworkers are saying at work, make sense of what is being said by those working with you on some projects, progress, process the information you have received, and make sound decisions based on it.

Managing people can be challenging because each person has their own quirks and communication styles. Dealing with this puts a lot of pressure on you, which could impact your attention to detail due to stress. However, if you have developed excellent and effective listening skills in the course of your life and studies, you will be able to play your part in the communication chain and deliver messages clearly.

Benefits of Effective Listening in Parenting

Parenting necessitates good listening skills for a variety of reasons. It's common knowledge that kids are never-ending chatterboxes because they constantly try to get their thoughts across and have no filters.

But within that stream of consciousness will be vital information you must not miss - don't tune out and let it become background noise. You must pay close attention until you understand what they are attempting to communicate to you, and this will, in turn, help you understand what they are saying and respond appropriately.

A good parent pays close attention to their children, not just to what they say but also to what they do – by reading their behavior. Therefore, listening helps you understand your children even beyond what they say.

The following are some of the ways that effective listening can improve your relationship with your children, which apply to both genders and ages:

1. Strengthening Your Relationship

Listening effectively to your children builds trust between you. They gain confidence in you because you can understand what upsets them. It also makes them easily confide in you. This strengthens your relationship and communication with them.

2. Conflict Resolution

Conflict resolution can be simple if you pay close attention to conversations. Listening effectively will help you understand differences from the children's perspectives, so you'll be able to react in a way that indicates you understand what's going on – and why – allowing you to address them appropriately.

Your children want to know that what they have previously said to you registered in your mind. You don't want to keep asking the same questions repeatedly because it will escalate the conflict.

If you listen to your kids closely enough, or anyone else in similar situations, for that matter, you can avoid arguments and build a better relationship with them.

3. Respect and Commitment

Effective listening demonstrates your love and concern for your children. Making them feel heard shows them you care, which builds commitment and respect in your relationship with them.

Effective Listening in Mentorship

If you are chosen to be someone's mentor, your listening skills will have to be sharpened. This is a position of responsibility and needs dedication. You need to make sure you listen carefully to your mentee, so good listening skills to be a good mentor. How essential is effective listening in mentoring? Let's cover that below.

3. Identifying Issues and Coming up with Solutions

Good listening skills will assist you in recognizing issues raised by your mentee, even if they have only expressed them nonverbally. You'll be able to decode those unspoken words, allowing you to search for and provide a solution. This is only possible if you pay close attention during conversations.

If you don't, you'll misunderstand your mentee, which could cause problems in your relationship because you won't be able to help solve problems or teach them what they need if you don't know their problems.

4. Building Trust between Both Mentor and Mentee

The relationship between a mentor and a mentee depends on many things, but trust is crucial. Mentees are more likely to be honest about their lives and struggles if they have confidence in you.

This trust, though, can't be built unless you have good listening skills, which will help them talk to you as they get to know you better over time.

5. Avoiding Conflicts Due to Communication Gaps

Conflicts are to be expected in all relationships, including those between mentors and mentees.

There may be times when you and your mentee have opposing viewpoints on specific issues. However, as the mentor, you have a responsibility to keep an open mind to their points of view and perspectives.

You will never understand their points of view if you are not a good listener.

You can encourage your mentee to share their thoughts and feelings by listening attentively and then asking leading questions. When you put yourself in their shoes, you gain a better understanding of their perspective and can use that to pave the way for more open lines of communication.

Listening Fosters Stronger Romantic Bonds

Listening is something that relationship specialists and therapists always emphasize. Unfortunately, many relationship problems can be traced back to a breakdown in any kind of communication in the relationship.

When people take the time to listen to each other, they create an environment where everyone feels comfortable sharing their thoughts and feelings without fear of criticism. Many troubled marriages experience this trouble because the partners have got into the habit of constantly cutting each other off and talking over one another, so this may take some time to change.

A trained couple's therapist may organize listening activities between couples to help with the process.

Listening Strengthens Friendships

Listening not only strengthens romantic and professional bonds but also strengthens friendships. If you're having trouble mending fences with longtime friends or connecting with new people, practicing active listening skills may be the answer.

Listening strengthens friendships by increasing trust, reducing misunderstandings, and increasing empathy. You should make an effort because it pays off.

Benefits of Effective Listening in Sales and Marketing

To be a successful salesman or marketer, good communication skills are a prerequisite, and your communication skills are not complete if you are not an effective listener.

One of your goals in communicating with potential customers and clients should be to gain insight into their needs and concerns concerning what you are selling and your products and services, as well as finding out information about your competitors' offerings and how you can use this information to improve your own offerings and attract more customers.

You won't be able to answer a question if you haven't read the situation in depth or listened adequately to your prospect's questions. Listening effectively to your prospective customers or clients has the following advantages:

- Your prospect will have faith in you because you have demonstrated that you value them by listening to them
- If the prospect discovers that you are more interested in meeting their needs than in making sales, they will be more willing to offer additional solutions and make necessary recommendations to you
- They will also be less reserved with you because you have shown your willingness to listen to them
- They believe in you and the solution that your products or services provided

- You can concentrate your efforts on those who genuinely require the product you provide

Remember that you are here to satisfy your customers as much as you are here to make sales. Therefore, listening effectively will reassure your customer that you care more about their satisfaction than your sales. This demonstrates to the customer that you genuinely care about their success, not just your own.

Show that you value every one of your customers. Give each of them the attention they need and make sure you personally attend to their needs and don't pass them off to someone else, as that is the quickest way to lose customers.

When you listen to each customer well enough, you'll make them feel that they are your top priority, which earns you their trust and commitment. Make no pretense about it. In all honesty, pay attention because if you don't, your client will find out, and you'll miss out on some information that may be crucial to your success in the long run.

Sometimes you already have a solution to a customer's problem. It is not a good idea to deny them the opportunity to express themselves because they will feel unimportant, and talk over them with your solution. Give them respect by giving them time to speak, and when they've finished, give them your response, but this time, modify it to fit what they've just described to you but echo some of the words they have used in their explanation.

Your effective listening skills will help you solve the same problem with different customers in different ways.

Effective listening will get you to reach an agreement quickly and unambiguously, providing solutions your customer is more likely to accept. If you can't listen, your sales rate will decrease, hurting your overall effectiveness – *and your pocket.*

Techniques for Effective Listening

1. Smiling

Smiling while listening to your speaker can help you listen more effectively. It assures the person speaking to you that they have your undivided attention and keeps you connected to them while they talk.

2. Leaning Forward

This is yet another effective listening technique. While someone is speaking to you, you adjust your posture to lean forward rather than sink back into your chair. When you lean forward, it's easier to block out background noise and concentrate on the speaker. It also gives them the impression that they have your full attention.

3. Eye Contact

Maintaining eye contact with the speaker while he is speaking is essential. This allows you to connect beyond the words they're saying. You can follow their gestures, facial expressions, and body language while they speak.

4. Paraphrasing the Speaker's Words

By attempting to paraphrase the speaker's words, you are already making sense of what they are saying, which dramatically improves your listening skills, as well as reassuring the person speaking to you that they have been heard.

5. Showing Concern

You can't show concern for the speaker if you don't follow up on the conversation. So, showing concern is beneficial to both you and the speaker. As you try to incorporate yourself into their narratives, it creates a bond and a sense of understanding between the two of you.

6. Asking for Clarification

Asking for clarification on ambiguous points is a great way to show that you're paying attention during a conversation or a chat. When something is not clear, be quick to ask for clarification, which, when provided, helps you understand what is being discussed better.

7. Summarizing

Your ability to summarize what has been said and pick the necessary points in the conversation is all part of effective listening. It helps you understand the message better and lets you build on it in your own way while keeping the main points in mind.

8. Acknowledging Verbally

During a conversation, verbal acknowledgment is vital to show that you are an effective listener. Verbal acknowledgment allows you to flow with the speaker as if you already know what he will say next. You're participating in the conversation and aren't missing anything, so you add a word to confirm something every now and then.

9. Highlighting Your Own Experiences

Finally, highlighting your own experience is on the list of techniques to improve effective listening. You can identify various points where the speaker said things that resonate with you as they speak.

How to Improve Your Listening Skills

Stick to a regular routine of reflection and contemplation. This will help you clear your mind and improve your concentration over time, which will reflect on your listening and communication methods.

Learn about the different types of listening and practice them regularly. Different types of listening include active listening, passive listening, critical listening, expansive listening, and reductive listening.

When you are in a noisy environment, try to listen to the different types of noise, figure them out one at a time, and isolate them. By doing so, you will acquire the ability to selectively tune out irrelevant sounds and maintain focus on the things you want to hear.

Find educational audio and video content and listen to it. This will significantly improve your listening skills while providing additional benefits such as education, motivation, etc. Check out things on YouTube, TV and radio shows, podcasts, etc.

You can do it while waiting for a train, driving, riding on the bus, or in any other spare moment.

Effective listening is a skill that will benefit you in many areas of your life. Developing this skill will have a hugely positive impact on your interpersonal relationships, and there are many lessons to be learned along the way. For example, you'll find out that you can't be an effective listener if you are doing all the talking. This teaches you to be quiet while listening, among other things.

When you let others speak before you respond, you can learn as much as possible about the topic and provide helpful feedback.

Keep an open mind when listening to pick out the critical details among the sea of spoken words. Don't let yourself get distracted too often, as it's possible that crucial information is being communicated just when you're about to lose focus.

Distractions can come in many forms, including off-topic conversations, interruptions from friends, and even cell phone ringing.

Keep your attention on the gestures and words, and jot down ideas as they come to you; you never know which one will come in handy.

Knowing that the message is more important than the messenger at that moment will help you improve. You could miss out on plenty of relevant details if you try to force the two together. Opportunity knocks when we realize that great ideas can come from people who may not share our values or beliefs.

Listening to responses or giving a counter-opinion is different from *listening to understand.* With the first type of listening, your mind is closed, only looking for the next opportunity to talk. But with the second, you have an open mind, you want to learn, and you want to learn essential things from what you hear.

In general, maintain your curiosity. Never close your mind to any issue; always be open to opposing viewpoints.

Knowing that your opinion on a subject may not be final will cause you to always ask questions that will enlighten you. It is not polite to interrupt people mid-sentence. It shows a lack of respect for the speaker and is very discouraging, and you risk losing sight of what is most important.

Be patient with those who may not be eloquent or quick with their words. Some people take longer than others to convey the same message. You should be aware of which applies to your speakers and give them the same value as anyone else.

Consistently demonstrate empathy and connection with your speaker. Demonstrate in your listening that you've processed the speaker's message and can relate to it. However, while showing empathy and connection, it is essential to maintain complete emotional control. Regardless of the speaker's attempts to push or pressure you with their words, you must maintain emotional control.

Always pay attention to body language while listening. Many things are communicated without words during a conversation, and you will miss them if you are not attentive enough.

If you put your mind to it, nothing is impossible to learn. In the same way, honing your existing skillset or learning new skills can have a significant impact.

Chapter 3: 5 Ways to Hear the Emotions behind the Words

Soft skills, such as effective communication, are highly valued in today's world and help improve cooperation and productivity in communities, workplaces, and at home. Global and local events have a way of distorting people's emotions and, in most cases, impair their ability to express themselves effectively. People frequently hide their true feelings behind a wall of words, making communication difficult.

Effective communication is more than just sharing information.
https://www.pexels.com/photo/pensive-ethnic-man-listening-to-answer-in-paper-cup-phone-3760607/

Words are an important part of our communication as humans, and expressing yourself, especially if you're in a vulnerable state, can be difficult. Notwithstanding, for effective communication to occur, any conversation must be founded on the pillars of empathy, emotional intelligence, and emotional awareness. To communicate, all parties must be able to understand themselves and others.

The speaker should be able to communicate their deepest feelings, and the listener should use logic to comprehend the message. Suppose the speaker appears to be hiding their emotions. In that case, the listener should be able to persuade the other party to communicate effectively by using emotional intelligence and emotional awareness.

Effective communication is more than just sharing information. The emotions behind the message must also be understood. Many things and so much outside noise can obstruct effective communication. The best results require a lot of effort.

This chapter examines how empathy, emotional awareness, and emotional intelligence affect the context of communication and how to understand people's expressions better.

Empathy, Emotional Awareness, Emotional Intelligence and Their Importance in Communication

Empathy is the ability to emotionally comprehend the feelings of others by viewing things from their point of view and imagining yourself in their situation. It means being aware of, sensitive to, and experiencing other people's thoughts and feelings. One can imagine themselves in the person's shoes and feel their emotions.

Emphatic people are good listeners, can recognize the feelings of others, are very helpful to people who find themselves in complex social situations, and provide excellent advice and assistance to those in need.

Empathy may be affective, somatic, or cognitive. Affective empathy is the ability to understand and respond appropriately to another person's feelings and emotions, whereas somatic empathy is the ability to have physical reactions in response to what another person is feeling. **Cognitive reaction** *is understanding and predicting another person's response to a situation.*

Empathy is instrumental in the context of communication. It enables you to communicate effectively with others because you understand and identify with them and can express yourself appropriately. Empathy facilitates forming of strong social bonds, which begin with meaningful conversations. It helps you moderate your emotions, which is beneficial in discussions because you'll then be able to communicate smoothly, even under different circumstances, such as when you're happy, stressed, or depressed, without pushing others away or imposing your opinions on them.

Emotional awareness is often confused with emotional intelligence; it comprises the ability to understand and recognize your own emotions and the emotions of others. It includes comprehending emotions and separating them, which aids communication.

People who are emotionally aware are good communicators because they understand their emotions and use them effectively to influence their conversations and ensure the message they want is communicated. They are aware of other people's emotions and communicate in a way that is reciprocal to those emotions.

Emotions are essential in communication, and awareness of them allows for effective communication. You will quickly learn to put measures in place to have progressive conversations. Most emotional responses can be predicted, and you can make better decisions because you know what actions are triggered by such emotions.

You will easily navigate and communicate your emotional phase, making communication easier and more fulfilling. Understanding one another is the heart of communication, and being aware allows you to do just that. It brings more joy and fulfillment. Thus incorporating this quality into a relationship or conversation makes communication more meaningful and memorable.

People with high emotional awareness have flourishing relationships because communication is always fluid and interesting. They can connect because they can converse openly and smoothly. They have done the work with themselves, which leads to a deep understanding of emotions – both theirs and their partner's, and if the relationship hits a rough patch, emotions can be confronted head-on so that the balance in the relationship is restored.

Emotional intelligence, like emotional awareness, refers to the ability to comprehend, apply, perceive, handle, and manage emotions. It is defined as a set of traits and skills that influence performance and leadership. It is the interface between your emotional and cognitive functions. And it's at this meeting point you can deduce people's emotions and respond appropriately.

It includes self-management, social awareness, and relationship management. Controlling impulsive behaviors, managing your emotions, knowing your limits, recognizing the feelings of others, understanding your own and their impact on others, being socially comfortable, inspiring great relationships, and clearly communicating with colleagues, friends, and those around you are all part of it.

It is a social skill that can be learned or inherited. It entails evaluating, recognizing, and controlling your own emotions and the emotions of others, using emotional information to guide behavior and thinking, discern and label different feelings, and shape them for adaptation to the environment.

People with high emotional intelligence are self-assured, curious, emphatic, sensitive, and concerned about others. They're reliable, admit mistakes and accept change. Emotionally intelligent people can communicate with sensitivity and understanding in their workplace and personal lives. Conflicts are unavoidable during conversations with people, and with emotional intelligence, you can effectively communicate in a way that resolves the conflict.

Understanding emotions help you to develop fruitful relationships with colleagues and acquaintances. Emotions influence communication, and understanding your feelings is integral to effective communication. Self-control is the ability to read situations and respond appropriately, and expressing yourself without aggression in stressful or uncomfortable situations are all emotional intelligence traits.

Emotional intelligence can improve teamwork and relationships in the workplace or family. It helps you discuss and reach compromises with opposing factions on various topics, generating togetherness. Evaluating your own and other people's emotions allows you to avoid conflicts, stay relaxed, and create a happy work team.

Being emotionally intelligent also lets you encourage and motivate people during difficult times; it gives you self-confidence, which allows you to approach people, assess situations, and provide helpful information to help them overcome their feelings. To achieve effective verbal and nonverbal communication, you must pay attention to emotions and words. Communication involves more emotion than information.

Empathy, emotional intelligence, and awareness are all skills that can help you communicate more effectively. They improve your ability to feel, control, use, and comprehend not only your own emotions but also the emotions of others. This is a valuable asset in families and workplaces, and developing these skills is critical in the context of communication.

5 Ways to Better Understand People's Expressions

Understanding people's expressions or the message they're conveying is essential to have productive conversations. Empathy allows you to put yourself in the shoes of others and see things from their perspective, while emotional awareness will enable you to read the situation, express yourself appropriately, and make tangible connections.

Using these skills individually or together facilitates emotional information and development. It enhances your ability to read meaning into the expressions and messages of others while attempting to persuade and lift their spirit. It takes a lot of effort to try to understand people. However, empathy, emotional intelligence, and emotional awareness can help.

Here are some strategies to help you understand what people may be trying to express:

1. Improved Self-Control with Emotional Intelligence

Being calm and in control of your emotions improves communication and allows you to see things from the perspective of others. Your feelings influence your communication, and controlling them will enable you to interact with others more effectively.

Emotional intelligence lets you control your thoughts, feelings, and utterances when under stress and helps you respond reflectively. It improves your self-control, prevents your emotions and nerves from getting the better of you, and instead of speaking quickly or aggressively, you remain calm and can hold reasonable conversations.

Understanding people's expressions at work requires emotional intelligence. Stress, workload, and pressure are common in the workplace. Responding inappropriately or misinterpreting a piece of information can lead to arguments, conflicts, or even work being undone. However, by exercising emotional intelligence, you can gain control of the situation, understand the feelings of others, and respond constructively. Understanding others makes you approachable and lets you influence their emotions. If you understand people, you can prevent or minimize conflicts, work through frustration, and foster happiness in the home or office. You get to cheer them up, talk through their emotions, and build better working relationships, which ultimately increases productivity.

2. Reading Situations

Emotional intelligence is the ability to decipher not only your own feelings but also those of others. Understanding other people's emotions and making sense of the environment around you makes it easier to reach compromises and productive solutions using effective and meaningful communication.

This implies self-regulation, listening, and responding in a conversation. You understand how to keep your responses convenient, subdue impulsive reactions, and slow down before expressing strong or critical opinions.

Reacting on impulse to the expressions of others creates a communication gap, which is unhealthy, while understanding how the other party feels, gaining insight into their mental or emotional state, attempting to put yourself in their shoes, or experiencing what they're going through allows you to make rational decisions. When you combine emotional intelligence and emotional awareness, you can better understand people.

When having a conversation with a friend who is experiencing anxiety, heartbreak, or loss, emotional intelligence advises you on the best course of action to take and reminds you to actively listen rather than bugging the person with your own concerns. You will be able to tell if the time is right to express your deepest feelings, a new idea, or a discovery during such conversations. You will know when and how to respond.

When a friend needs someone to listen to them, it's going to be emotional intelligence that will help you to determine whether you should speak or just listen. It enables you to assess the situation, adapt to it, and provide an appropriate solution to the conversation. You will understand when to participate and when to remain silent during a conversation. You will avoid conflict, prevent issues from exacerbating, and be diplomatic in your dealings with others.

3. Empathy and Understanding

Empathy entails relating to and comprehending the emotions of others. Viewing things from the perspective of others and attempting to experience how they feel improves communication and relationships in homes, offices, and colleges. Empathy is essential in communication. It entails comprehending the circumstances of others and the feelings that the situation may elicit in the individual. After identifying what a person is attempting to express or what they are experiencing, the next step is to try to relate to that situation.

Cultivate empathy, as it's crucial to understand what is happening with other people and think like them. To be effective at helping others, you need to observe their words and actions. If you work at the same place, look at their working conditions or attitude to work, ask emphatic questions to find out what's causing the trouble, try to understand how they feel, and get them to talk more about the situation.

If your boss or a colleague exhibits irritable behavior at work, don't react similarly. Instead, figure out what's wrong, try to understand how they're feeling, and offer assistance as needed and appropriate. To understand people, you must put yourself in their shoes and see things from their perspective. This allows you to assist them and interact more suitably. With empathy, you can avoid conflicts and set realistic expectations for yourself and your relationship with your boss, colleague, or friend.

4. Reflection before Reaction

Emotions influence how you perceive, understand, handle, and respond to others. Understanding other people's emotions requires us to empathize before taking action or offering a solution relevant to that situation. Combining empathy, emotional intelligence, and emotional awareness allows you to read, relate, and respond to a situation appropriately and on time.

Human emotions are a tangled web for anyone to navigate, but getting to the point between mental and emotional functionality allows you to see what's going on before taking action. To fully understand what others are feeling, you must first master your own emotions. Taking control of your own emotions prevents you from being aggressive, demanding, or unhelpful to the person you are talking to, and understanding the emotions of others makes it easier to help them.

You will be able to detect and collect emotional and mental data, examine and interpret it, and then be helpful with a proper response. You will be able to think about what is in front of you and respond appropriately. You'll know when it's appropriate to respond or remain passive while listening and offering assistance as needed.

5. Build Trust

Effective communication cannot occur without trust. Building trust with the individual lays the groundwork for a good conversation. Looking at things through their eyes and getting them to open up can only happen if there is trust. You never know how far something as simple as a handshake can go. Making eye contact, and sitting beside or in front of the person, can help you to start a conversation.

Since you can put yourself in their shoes and emotional intelligence allows you to predict the emotions which may lead to a specific action, talk to them as if you are in the same situation. If you've been there, describe your experience and how you overcame it. Trust is essential to understand others, so be careful not to lose it as you build your social and work circles.

Recognizing flaws and mistakes can occur when understanding people keeps the conversation moving. Helping the person understand that mistakes do happen can also assist them in admitting their feelings, opening up, and having those difficult conversations.

Misunderstandings occur at work, at home, and even with friends, but they can be avoided if you use your emotional intelligence. A colleague may be angry over past events, or a child or teacher may have annoyed a family member, who then acted out against you. With emotional intelligence, you can reflect on your response and agree that a past event or circumstance may have caused that behavior while fully understanding that you have done nothing wrong to warrant that degree of reaction. Understanding emotions greatly helps effective communication. Demonstrating care, empathy, and intelligence when dealing with emotional conversations and situations also helps communication.

How to Improve Relationally and Evaluate the Emotions of Others

Developing emotionally and attempting to deduce the emotions others hide behind their words is a difficult task. Emotional skills are extremely beneficial, and while they can be innate, they can also be learned. With consistent practice and dedication, you can substantively read meaning into the messages and expressions of others.

Exercises for emotional development and emotion deduction include:

Practicing Mindfulness

Your mind is a vast space that houses your thoughts, feelings, and emotions. Thus, learning how to comprehend and focus on a specific event will help you understand others. It will be easier to relate to others if you can train your mind to focus on the present moment, pay attention to a conversation, and not make snap judgments.

Mindfulness is how you appreciate different moments in life and experience physical and mental sensations. It allows you to remain calm, see things from a different perspective, and stay focused. You'll be able to control your emotions and those of others by practicing mindfulness.

Prioritize Listening

Active listening is the most effective way to read emotional messages from people. Keep your mind open and present in the conversation while actively listening to what the other person has to say. You can't help someone if you don't know what's wrong, and you can't know what's wrong if you don't listen. When a friend calls to express their dismay or frustration, you can't hear the emotions behind the words spoken if you're distracted.

You can also put yourself in their shoes if they contact you via text, and you should try to read their intent. Look for verbal cues such as voice tones or nonverbal cues during conversations. If they insist they're fine and have things under control, take their word for it but follow up with subsequent conversations.

Explore Differences

You can't give good advice if you have a rigid mindset and lifestyle. You'll tell them to be like you rather than assisting them by seeing beyond their emotions. Investigate other cultures, solicit other people's opinions, try out new things and always be curious.

Try to see or experience things from their perspective. You don't want to help someone and then be told, "You don't know what it's like." You may not have grown up or experienced things the same way they did, but having an idea, insight, or inkling of what it's like to be them can help you understand others.

Offer Help

Putting yourself in the person's shoes or feeling their pain isn't enough on its own. Try to lift them up as well. Feelings are nice, but they aren't enough. What matters is what you do. Take the risk if you can provide physical assistance to alleviate the pain, stress, or discomfort.

To lighten the mood and reduce the burden, use humor and laughter, which are natural stress antidotes. Empathy and emotional awareness are useful, but if you can offer assistance, the person will likely appreciate it more.

Communication is more about emotions than information, so understanding emotions is essential to effective communication. It is difficult to discuss emotions and how they affect our everyday communication, and understanding how our moods, feelings, and states of mind can be expressed or concealed behind words or other forms of expression can improve or degrade communication.

Empathy, emotional awareness, and emotional intelligence all play important roles in communication. Using them can help you understand the emotions expressed in other people's words. You must be able to handle, manage, and perceive your own emotions and the emotions of others, all while using emotional awareness and emotional intelligence to control your thoughts and potential responses to a situation.

Emotional development aims to achieve this by paying attention not only to words but also to the genuine message conveyed within statements made. Being emotionally sound, aware, and responsible to others facilitates better relationships and conversations.

Paying attention, actively listening, and being mindful of your response are all strategies to employ. It is not enough to feel and experience the pain of others. You must also build trust and, when necessary, take action. Only then can you fully realize the potential of effective communication.

Chapter 4: How Body Language Can Make or Break a Conversation

We have been told time and time again to "Think before we speak," but merely following this golden principle is highly unlikely to lead to fruitful conversations. Words constitute only around 30% of the message conveyed in a conversation, and 70% of what is absorbed by the listener depends on your body language and tone of voice. So, choosing the right words is only a small part of the equation.

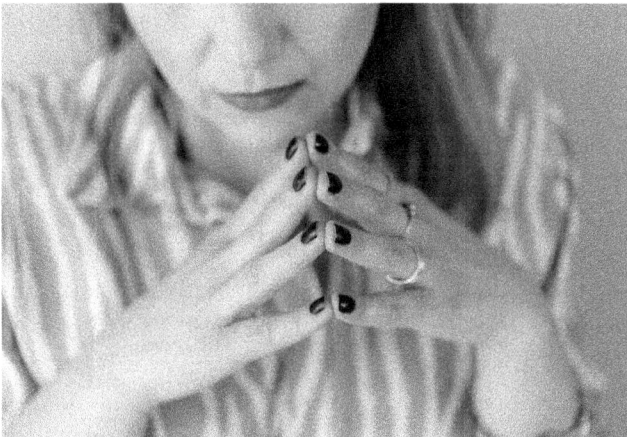

Body language includes all the non-verbal cues.
https://www.pexels.com/photo/woman-with-steepled-fingers-7320508/

Body language is the silent form of communication that plays a vital role in a conversation. It includes all the non-verbal cues, gestures, posture, facial expressions, and tone as well. Body language conveys more than words.

Impact of Body Language

It is a little alarming that body language plays such a huge part in communication, yet we are mostly unaware of what our body is doing while speaking. Bad body language is off-putting, offensive, and sometimes hurtful. It is also necessary to actively learn to understand and practice positive non-verbal cues to have more pleasant conversations.

Body language helps us to understand others and express ourselves in a better way. You can understand the emotions and thoughts in a person's head through body language. For instance, a tilted head and direct eye contact can show that the person is interested in the conversation and listening carefully.

Body language can help you understand people better and build strong relationships with them. It can also help you interpret someone's reaction to something you're saying. For instance, if someone frowns at you, it means that they are angry or don't agree with your opinions. Your body language can be intentional or unintentional, positive or negative. Once you learn more about it, you can eliminate unintentional negative traits and intentionally incorporate positive ones. Learning about body language can help you communicate effectively and make you more confident and appealing.

How Body Language Can Be a Communication Barrier

Body language can become a communication barrier because it speaks more than words do. For instance, if someone is talking about a sensitive matter, and you say, "I'm listening," but you don't exhibit any facial expressions to back up your words, chances are there that they won't believe you and may stop talking to you. Suppose it's apparent from your body language that you're nervous or anxious. In that case, people may find this off-putting enough to avoid talking to you. A person who avoids eye contact, keeps their head down, and has a slouchy posture will be considered disinterested in the conversation. However, positive body language attracts people to start communicating with you and to continue to communicate.

Types of Non-Verbal Communication

1. **Facial expressions** are the first thing that a person will see while talking to you. If your expressions make you seem disinterested, there's no way that your words will assure the other person that you're really interested.

2. **Gestures** - Waving your hand to say hello is a kind gesture. You can also use gestures to support your words, such as a thumbs up when you agree to something.

3. **Eye contact** -Making eye contact can emphasize your presence. Rolling your eyes is a sign of displeasure or irritation. The eyes are a window to one's soul and can express a lot.

4. **Posture** - Your posture can indicate your comfort level, self-esteem, confidence, and interest in the conversation.

5. **Proxemics** -The use of distance while communicating.

6. **Paralanguage** -This includes how you talk, tone, speaking speed, pitch, and loudness.

7. **Haptics** -This refers to the body language which involves touch, such as hugging, handshakes, and holding hands.

How to Interpret Emotions from One's Body Language

You can read a person's body language from the different parts of the body, including their eyes, hands, face, and feet. Observing all these and coming to a conclusion is better than interpreting something by looking at a single part. Sometimes a person may not be able to express what he wants to, but his body language will get his message across.

For instance, if your friend is telling you that he's fine, but his eyes are watery, his tone is shaky, and he's not smiling, then you may conclude that he's upset about something but isn't comfortable sharing it. You can encourage him to share his problems with you and make him realize that you won't judge him; you'll simply listen to him with empathy, which may help him open up to you and build a better bond.

Facial expressions alone can show so much about what a person is feeling, and that's why they're considered a universal form of communication. Eminent American researcher and psychologist Paul Ekman has published plenty of papers on the subject to confirm how important facial expressions are to communication.

Even if there was no language, you would still be able to understand other person's emotions through their facial expressions. A smiling face shows happiness, while frowning is a sign of sadness. Anger, fear, confusion, excitement, and desire are all emotions that can be understood just by observing facial expressions.

Other body parts also play a vital role in understanding emotion. Think about a person sitting beside you, constantly biting his nails and shaking his legs. You would be able to understand that he's either stressed or anxious. There wasn't a single exchange of words between you, but you understood his state of mind by observing his body language. That shows the importance of body language in understanding feelings, emotions, and moods.

Positive Non-Verbal Cues

Often, we're unaware of our non-verbal communication through our body movements, gestures, and posture. By knowing more about positive non-verbal cues, you can incorporate these consciously into your daily life. It will help you communicate better and leave a remarkable first impression of your personality with those who meet you.

These are some of the most important examples of positive non-verbal cues.

1. Good Posture

A good posture conveys that you are not nervous, anxious, or confused. To maintain good posture, be mindful of your head, shoulders, and back position. Keeping your head high, shoulders relaxed, and back straight will make you look comfortable and confident.

2. Leaning In

It is important to keep your back straight when you are talking because it shows confidence. However, when the other person is talking, leaning in a little is a proven way of showing interest and empathy. You can make the speaker more comfortable by leaning in because this sends out a message that you are totally invested in the conversation.

3. Eye Contact

This is not an easy one. Too little or too much of it can ruin the entire conversation. Breaking eye contact every now and then so that it doesn't look like you are staring is part of effective communication and conversation.

4. Arms

Crossing your arms in front of you is like holding up a shield to defend yourself from attack. This gesture indicates that you could be scared and defensive and are ready to finish the conversation as soon as possible. If this is not the message you wish to convey, hang your arms comfortably by your side. If you are sitting, bringing your hands together in your lap is a good way to show interest and eagerness.

How to Appear Confident

A straight posture is an essential positive non-verbal cue that can help you appear confident. If you slouch and cross your arms or legs, try to get out of this habit, as it indicates social anxiety and makes you appear less confident. Don't put your hands in your pockets and look down while speaking/walking because those gestures also make you appear anxious and nervous. If you have a habit of moving your legs, biting your nails, or shaking your knees, try to control them. It won't be easy at first, but it'll enhance your personality and make you appear more confident.

Always make eye contact while listening or speaking because it shows that you're paying attention and are interested in the conversation. Making eye contact while speaking is a sign that you feel confident and positive about the subject you are discussing.

Always shake hands firmly - not too tight and not too open. This may be simple, but it can reveal a lot about your personality. Slow down your movements when you move forward to shake hands, as fast and vigorous movements can be interpreted as anxiety.

The appropriate tone of voice is a crucial positive non-verbal cue. It's not what you say, but it is how you speak. You can lift your communication skills by working on your tone, pitch, and pauses between your words.

Positive nonverbal cues show you're interested in the conversation.

Head Nodding

If you nod your head whenever you agree with another person's point of view, it'll show that you're paying attention. Nodding your head with a smile indicates that you're interested and enthusiastic about the conversation.

Open Palms

Open palms say that you're not defensive but are open to whatever the other person is saying. It means you're receiving their opinion and ideas openly without any defensiveness.

Leaning Forward

Leaning forward in a conversation is interpreted as a sign of engagement and interest in the conversation. It shows that you want to hear the speaker better.

Making Eye Contact

Eye contact can make the speaker feel that they're being heard. Although making eye contact is really important, don't do it to the extent that it starts to make the other person feel uncomfortable.

Positive Non-Verbal Cues That Show Empathy

Relaxed Face

A relaxed face can show that you have a soft personality. Softness is the key to empathy. Keep stern looks for when you mean to be stern, and look gently at the other person. Smile more often to look more approachable.

Eyebrows

Your eyebrows can express a lot. While listening to someone, lifting your eyebrows can show that you're actually concerned about them. It shows that you're right there with them.

Voice

Your soft tone can do a lot more than you think. Speaking slowly and in a soft tone is a sign that you're gentle, calm, and caring.

Breathing

You may have noticed that your breathing changes during different emotions. When you're angry or frustrated, you'll find you breathe quicker. Try to breathe slowly, deeply, and calmly. It shows that you have a relaxed personality.

Use of Hands

You can use your hands while listening to others to show empathy. For instance, if someone is anxious, nervous, or stuck with a problem, you can hold and squeeze their hand to show that you want to be there for them. Putting a hand on someone's shoulder during a conversation also shows that you have a friendly personality.

Mirroring

Mirroring is basically copying/mimicking the other person's body language, tone, posture, etc. It shows that you're interested and totally engaged in the conversation. For instance, matching their tone, pace, and volume will show that you have the same energy and vibe. Mirroring is a form of active communication because when someone sees a reflection of himself in another person's actions, he automatically develops trust and gets comfortable being around them. Don't overdo it.

Negative Non-Verbal Cues

Negative non-verbal cues include gestures, postures, and expressions that may offend others or hurt and decrease your influence and respect. These can be intentional or unintentional. Negative non-verbal cues can affect your personal as well as professional life.

The following is a list of nonverbal cues that you need to avoid.

Maintaining Distance

Maintaining a certain healthy distance while communicating is really crucial. While communicating, it should never feel like you're invading the other person's personal space.

Check Your Facial Expressions

Sometimes we're unaware of the facial expressions we're giving to others. Negative facial expressions can really break up a conversation. Controlling your facial expressions is quite a tough job, but you can learn to do it by practicing in front of a mirror. You need to keep your face straight and relax. Loosen up your jaw and relax your forehead.

Constantly Touching Your Face and Hair

This may seem a harmless habit, but it shows that you're distracted and not interested in the conversation, hence finding ways to distract yourself. You may find this habit difficult to overcome, but being aware of it – and working on it gradually – will help you to stop it.

Covering Your Mouth

Covering your mouth during a conversation can show that you're either anxious or don't have confidence. Most people do that while being in group discussions, whether personal or professional office meetings.

Eye Contact

Avoiding eye contact can be interpreted as low confidence, lack of self-esteem, or fear due to lying. People don't look into someone else's eyes when they lie, so it could be misinterpreted if you have difficulty with this. However, it is considered disrespectful in some cultures, so you must judge depending on the situation.

Too much eye contact, i.e., staring, is also a negative non-verbal cue because it makes the other person uncomfortable.

Crossed Arms

This is known as a sign of either defensiveness or discomfort. It creates a barrier between you and the person you're communicating with. It either shows that you're uncomfortable or don't agree with their thoughts.

Hand Movements

Too many fast hand or body movements show you're anxious or nervous. Sweating while making a conversation is also a sign of anxiety.

Looking Away

Looking away at various objects (such as wall clocks and paintings) or constantly checking your phone can annoy the person you're communicating with. He may think that you're not interested in the conversation.

How Can Non-Verbal Communication Go Wrong?

How you communicate through your body language affects how people see you. You may add non-verbal cues unintentionally, but people don't ignore them. Sometimes you think you're doing everything right, but things go wrong because of those unintentional non-verbal cues. Below are some examples of how non-verbal communication can go wrong:

1. Jane is young, beautiful, and a smart woman. She has a good sense of humor and gets along with everyone. But still, she isn't able to build a long-term relationship or friendship because she constantly moves her legs, bites her nails, and has violent hand movements. She is constantly anxious, and anyone who's around her feels that too.

2. Simon is an empathetic person, he thinks he gets along with everyone in the office, but if you ask his co-workers, they don't agree with that because they find him to be too intense. He doesn't maintain a healthy distance and invades everyone's private space. While shaking hands, he holds the other person's hand so firmly that it makes them feel uncomfortable.

3. Mike is a young boy who tries to be friendly but still doesn't have any friends. He can initiate friendships but can't make them last. This is because Mike's face turns red whenever someone gives his opinion, and his facial expressions show that he doesn't agree with them. This pushes everyone away from him.

4. Alexa congratulated Megan on her promotion, but Megan noticed the jealousy and sadness in her tone. So Megan could interpret that Alexa wasn't happy with her success.

Minor details that you do subconsciously play an important role in forming your image to those observing you.

How to Develop Better Non-Verbal Communication

Here are some tips that can be used in daily life to gradually develop your non-verbal communication skills:

Observe Yourself

You need to observe yourself and keep noticing all the unintentional non-verbal cues you use in your everyday life. Think about your normal posture and tone and how it changes during different emotions such as anger, sadness, and nervousness. Assess what needs to be changed and work on that.

Avoid Using Incompatible Non-Verbal Cues

Do you say that you're fine while moving your legs? This is a sign that you're giving mixed messages. The other person will understand that you're actually not fine but trying to hide your feelings.

Learn from Others

Observe what kind of non-verbal cues others use in order to express themselves or while making a conversation. For instance, if there's a confident person, you can watch him for cues that make him seem that way and try to copy them.

There's No Hard and Fast Rule

There's no strict rule that a certain non-verbal cue means a specific thing. The meaning of non-verbal cues can vary according to personal and cultural aspects. You need to ask before you assume. For instance, if someone is looking down while talking to you, you may ask him if he does that by habit or if something is upsetting him.

Relationship between Confidence and Body Language

Amy Cuddy is a Harvard University researcher who studied body language and its effect on confidence. According to her research, relaxed and open body language or high-power poses should boost confidence more than a closed and stiff body. High power poses increase testosterone and decreases cortisol, ultimately boosting confidence. Many people practice high-power poses in the morning to keep their confidence up throughout the day. Keeping your posture right the whole day will add up so much to your confidence levels.

Some common nonverbal interpretations:

- **Leaning towards a person:** This mostly shows that one is interested in the conversation but is sometimes interpreted as aggression.

- **Avoiding eye contact:** Can be interpreted as shyness, lack of confidence, no self-esteem, and even fear.

- **Crossing arms or legs:** Is mostly seen as defensiveness, but some people do it because they're nervous or because it is a habit.

- **Shaking/moving legs:** A sign of nervousness, anxiety, or boredom.

- **Forming a fist:** This shows aggression in most cases, but some people may do it because they feel threatened.

- **Eye roll:** Irritation, annoyance, or boredom.

Although understanding body language and learning how to interpret the common body language helps boost communication skills, there are no strict rules about these. It can vary according to the situation. For instance, putting a hand on someone's shoulder in the workplace could be considered a bad sign, but if you do that at a friend's meetup, it may be considered a friendly gesture. In the same way, this can also vary from person to person. Some people bite their nails because it's a habit and not due to anxiety or nervousness. If you're confused about someone's body language, you can always ask questions to help you to understand better. You can look at a person's body language as a whole instead of looking at individual signals to come to a better conclusion. For example, suppose someone is leaning forward, and you don't know whether he's doing that because he's interested or aggressive. In that case, you can observe the truth by looking at his facial expressions. If he's leaning forward while smiling, he's obviously interested in you and the conversation.

Good body language is not something you are born with or without. It is something you can learn, practice, and perfect. Having an important conversation without understanding and practicing positive non-verbal cues is like doing a plank without engaging your core. The former will hurt your muscles, and the latter will hurt your relationships.

Chapter 5: How to Spark up a Conversation...with Anyone

What better way to express yourself and help others understand you than through communication?

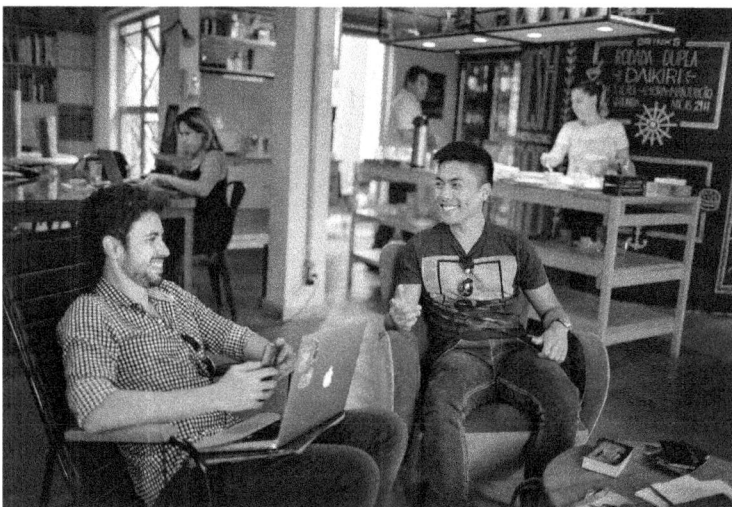

A great conversation can lead to both participants learning new things and give them wonderful memories to look back on in the future.

Even if you are an introvert, there are strategies you can employ to make any conversation easier. Striking up conversations with strangers can be very challenging, especially if you don't feel confident or have no interesting way to engage them.

All of your concerns and assumptions appear to be based solely on what is in your head. Starting a conversation is simple if you understand the person's personality well.

A great conversation can lead to both participants learning new things and give them wonderful memories to look back on in the future.

The key to success in social interactions like this is to develop some outstanding conversation starters that you can use to spark engaging conversations with anyone, whether in a business or social setting.

Watch the mood of the people around you and pick your moment to begin a conversation. By observing people, you can read the social cues and then be able to initiate a conversation. Choose your time carefully so you don't mess up your first impression on others.

How Communication Can Help You Build Social Relationships

Having good relationships with people lessens feelings of stress and anxiety. Your mental health will be in jeopardy, and your anxiety will increase if your relationships with others are unhealthy. This can cause you to avoid social situations and prevent you from developing positive relationships.

When you desperately want to make friends or meet new people but are afraid to make the first move, you can start to feel anxiety and mental stress.

The disadvantage of avoiding social relationships is that you will not be able to develop the confidence that comes from interacting with others. You won't be able to develop good communication skills that could have increased your chances of having successful relationships.

For example, suppose you are afraid of going on a date with someone, perhaps due to a lack of confidence or experience. In that case, you will be unable to handle situations such as knowing what to say or wear. You almost certainly have the ability but lack the confidence to put it to use. Below are some tips for starting a conversation.

Best Way to Initiate a Conversation

The first step toward developing a healthy social relationship is communicating your intentions and opinions, which do not have to be verbal. The vast majority of our interactions are non-verbal. Anyone who pays attention to your body language will generally pick up on your message.

A deaf person will get your message simply by watching your eye movements and other body language cues. You should be mindful of the signals your body sends out in social situations, as they could be interpreted in ways you didn't intend.

On the plus side, verbal and non-verbal communication skills can help you share knowledge, ideas, suggestions, and other valuable information with others, allowing you to form stronger bonds with them.

Communication is essential for social bonding; an easy way to start a conversation is by complimenting others. Make it about them or a random interesting topic instead of yourself. Allow others to speak and be a good listener because no one enjoys talking to someone who isn't attentive. If you show that you can accept and even appreciate different points of view, you'll encourage more conversation and gain the respect of your peers and anyone you interact with.

Communication makes you feel less anxious, improves your ability to talk to others, boosts your confidence, and lets you learn from others.

Strategies for Initiating Conversation with Strangers

Throughout your life, you will encounter different people in various settings. Knowing how to start a conversation with these new acquaintances can be difficult.

When you succeed in starting a conversation on a positive note, it can develop into something more interesting. Most of the time, we only have one chance to engage a stranger in conversation, and if we mess up that opportunity, everything else is ruined.

How you communicate with a stranger in an office differs from how you would communicate with someone in a grocery store.

Different scenarios dictate specific approaches. Starting a conversation with a stranger can be awkward, so you should know where and when to begin.

- Don't waste the stranger's time. Keep the conversation brief if you notice they are preoccupied.

Maintain your cool and confidence as you make the bold move of starting a conversation. Take a deep breath, and organize your thoughts. It won't look good if the stranger sees that you are nervous.

1. Keep a positive attitude and refrain from using body language that contradicts your intentions. Maintain eye contact and act friendly, as this will demonstrate that you are friendly and confident.

2. You can start with a question about something you have in common, such as the news, the weather, or their lunch choice - your situation will influence your subject. Consider questions or comments you can make about the subject as they respond to keep the conversation going.

3. Compliments work like magic when approaching strangers because most people enjoy being admired. You could say something like, "I really like your shoes." This complement may spark further conversation about the shoes. You must follow up with additional questions, such as whether other colors are available and where they purchased them. Not everyone will be willing to answer additional questions from you, but regardless of their response, keep a positive attitude.

4. Use something in your immediate surroundings to start a conversation. If you're in a restaurant, point to your favorite spot and invite the stranger to try it out.

5. You could also ask, "Do you live in this neighborhood? I saw your car pass mine the other day."

6. Do you want to keep things simple? Then you should start with an introduction. "Hello, my name is ... I recently moved into the neighborhood, and I come here every Friday to play tennis. I hope to see you around." This has given you some ideas for your next meeting. Remember that you're talking to a

stranger, so don't tell them too much about yourself straight away to avoid boring them. Allow them to talk about themselves as well.

7. Help someone you don't know. Helping a stranger carry a box or bag is an ideal time to strike up a conversation. As you help them, ask them questions like, "Did you just move in here?" When you offer to help a stranger, and they say yes, use the opportunity to ask them other questions that don't involve you.

8. Be open to hearing other people's views. If you're out for lunch and can't decide which chicken dish to try, you can ask them which one they prefer. Continue the conversation with related topics, and possibly ask to sit with them if they don't mind.

9. Keep up with current events and use a viral topic to start a conversation. As they respond, other interesting topics will emerge, and the conversation will flow.

10. Asking for assistance is also a good way to start a conversation. When you are new to a situation, ask for help with what you don't know or understand, and take advantage of the opportunity to start a great conversation.

11. When you meet people who share your interests, take advantage of the opportunity to discuss them, remembering to let them lead the conversation at first. This is a great way to get them excited about talking to you.

12. Make a remark that shows you have noticed the stranger. Say something like, "I noticed you write with your left hand. I am also left-handed." This will make the stranger feel more at ease and possibly open to further conversation.

13. When starting a conversation with a stranger, you can use your good sense of humor to make the stranger laugh. Tell jokes that aren't offensive and which are relevant to what's going on in your current location. Having a great sense of humor makes it easier to make friends and get along with others.

Tips for Making a Good First Impression

The importance of first impressions in forming social relationships cannot be overstated. What you communicate carries less weight than how you communicate.

Someone can form an opinion about you based on a single incidence of eye contact.

You may argue that judging people so quickly is unfair, and you may be right, but we're dealing with reality here, and assumptions are unavoidable. People who look at you will make many assumptions about you.

Some people cling to first impressions for far too long, despite everything. They believe their initial assessment is the most accurate and are adamant that they won't change their opinion. People having a negative first impression of you can ruin their potential relationship with you.

People use first impressions to filter characteristics in others that will be remembered in subsequent interactions. You'll hear things like, "I've always known you can't be trusted since the first time I laid eyes on you." It's difficult to change that first impression if it's not positive, so try to always make your first impression a positive and memorable one.

The persistence of first impressions can be attributed to our subconscious nature. Even when presented with contradicting evidence, our cognitive and implicit biases prevent us from revising our initial assessment.

You can think of first impressions as social capital that you can use to strengthen your bonds with others. Making a positive first impression can lead to new opportunities, especially if your experience and qualifications are a good fit.

Even if you are scared, act confidently to give the impression that you are confident. People will be drawn to you if you appear confident.

The following tips will help you to make a good first impression.

Appear Confident

When you are around people, your responsibility is to provide value; the only way to do so is to research and learn. Basic research on your surroundings will influence your decision on how to dress and whether bad language is acceptable. Preparing ahead of time will make you feel more at ease and show your focus and interest.

Give Emotional Support

Paying attention to the other person's emotions demonstrates your empathy. Emotional support will not only help you make a good first impression, but it will also help you form a strong connection with the other person. It shows that you care, and they will believe you are a loving person.

Good Body Language

Maintain positive body language because people can misinterpret it if you are slightly off. Deaf people rely heavily on non-verbal cues like facial expressions and gestures to make meaning of a conversation. Sit up straight and hold your head up to show confidence and comfort. Cross your legs and place your arms on your lap. As a welcoming gesture, offer a firm, though non-harmful, handshake.

Talk Less and Listen More

Be an excellent communicator who listens more and speaks less. To keep this going, make sure you talk less than half as much as you listen. Listening more demonstrates that you are attentive and love hearing about the other party. Making others feel good by listening well and communicating clearly is important.

Be Real

You are the best version of yourself, so stay true to yourself. It is easy to identify a fake, and you certainly wouldn't want that associated with your reputation. Simply be yourself and avoid attempting to prove a point during the first impression because this will come across as being insecure. Know your own weaknesses and strengths, and communicate them with care.

Dress Well

Isn't it true that the way you dress determines how you'll be addressed? People will make many assumptions about you based on what you wear. Whether you believe it or not, there are consequences for what you wear. For example, if you go to a job interview and dress casually, it will be assumed that you will not take the job seriously.

Smile Genuinely

A great first impression begins with a smile. People feel welcome and at ease around you when you wear a genuine smile. Don't force it because eyes don't lie. When you smile genuinely, it shows in your eyes and gives the impression that you are sincere and trustworthy.

Maintain Eye Contact

Eye contact is a nonverbal communication technique that shows respect for the person you are speaking with. Maintaining eye contact demonstrates that you are paying attention. Look the other person in the eyes before starting the conversation, and continue to do so throughout the conversation. Do not confuse staring at someone with correct eye contact.

Be Suggestive

If it's an official meeting, research the person and company to get a sense of what they're all about. Making informed contributions during a conversation will go a long way in demonstrating your commitment. Don't give your opinion too quickly. Instead, be suggestive so you don't make things worse or send the wrong message.

Bring a notebook to jot down notes if it's a business meeting. You don't want to be perceived as disengaged, so write something down even if you can remember it without writing it down.

Use Light Humor

A good sense of humor will help you to network with people in a less tense manner. Making them laugh or smile before you market your product is an excellent way to make a good first impression. Sarcasm should be avoided because it can backfire. Remember, you're talking to a stranger and have no idea how sensitive they are, so keep the jokes light.

Tell a Story

Another way to relax and focus on the people around you is to tell them a story. Use the story-telling format to sell yourself and your business, and include humorous experiences to make the story stand out and become memorable. Your story can take any form, be it advice, guidance, or education, but make sure it's laced with humor to keep it entertaining.

Pay Attention

A good communicator is also a good observer, so pay attention to finding something in common with the other person and use that to start a conversation. Don't present yourself as knowing it all, as this may be intimidating to some people, causing them to avoid you. And being a know-it-all is never attractive so let people join the debate before you kill it with your opinions.

Make the conversation about the other person rather than yourself. People will think you're arrogant and only want to show off if you put the spotlight on yourself. Make the conversation about how others will benefit from what you are saying, and you will notice that they will pay attention until you are finished.

Stop trying to be right, especially when dealing with someone you've just met. Being defensive and confrontational will destroy the relationship before it even begins.

Speak Properly and Clearly

People will judge you based on your speaking style, which is the first verbal expression they will receive from you. Your words and tone of your voice will be used to assess your leadership ability, cultural value, and intelligence. Mumbling is a sign of weakness. Instead, speak clearly to be heard. Combine your pitch with a flawless facial expression that shows what you're saying without hiding your intentions.

How to Master Small Talk to avoid Lacking What to Say

Isn't it amazing how some people can meet strangers and strike up a conversation that lasts for hours with no dull moments? They can accomplish this with a series of smaller conversations known as small talk.

Small talk will help you engage in a conversation with anyone without feeling awkward or making the person uncomfortable. Mastering the art of small talk will improve your networking skills, and you'll get to form lasting friendships.

Some people are antisocial, and no matter how much you try to compliment or question them, they will ignore you. Instead of feeling bad, bid them farewell and leave with a positive attitude. Just say, "All right, it was nice chatting with you. I'm off to meet my friends. I'll see you another time." If they aren't interested, let it go.

Small talk is intended to be uncontroversial and polite, so avoid discussing war, religion, politics, and similarly sensitive topics. Talking about such topics may end up increasing the distance between you two.

Certain in-depth discussions, such as those involving death, conspiracy theories, the end of the world, and those mentioned above, can make those around you feel uneasy. Avoid bringing up sensitive topics in the guise of small talk.

To keep the conversation going, build on your small talk or find related topics. For example, if you compliment someone's clothing and they appreciate it, you can ask where they purchased it or if you can order it online. Then you can move on to discussing matching shoes for such a dress, always leaving room for them to contribute more than you do in the conversation.

Drive the conversation, but let the other person keep it going with their opinion. Conversations are threads of related topics that can come from you or the other person. Be willing to listen to other people's stories.

Questions are excellent ways to learn new things but keep them relevant to the situation at hand. Digression from the topic could be interpreted as a lack of interest, and the other party may also become disinterested.

Instead of trying to sound interesting during small talk, be interested. Make it clear to the other person that you are paying attention to them. Small talk does not imply that you should entertain others by talking about yourself and other irrelevant topics; rather, you should be able to discuss related, friendly topics that are engaging for both parties.

You can ask emotional questions, such as what they like best about a city or your current environment. This should pique their interest enough so they will express themselves.

Pauses will happen, and it will be awkward. But don't be put off by them. Let them settle before speaking again. Don't force a conversation, no matter how much you want to say.

Finally, make small talk a habit. The only way to master this act is to practice with people on a bus, in a store, with colleagues, neighbors, and anyone else.

Tips for Introverts to Stay Engaged in Conversation

Conversations in a social setting begin with small talk and can progress to something deeper if both parties desire it.

When you first meet someone, it's not a good idea to bring up a personal subject like where they live and if they are in a relationship. The person you are speaking to could see your interest as too probing and uncomfortable.

Have a collection of conversation starters on hand, such as a compliment, a request, or asking random relatable questions, to use in various situations.

Asking them about themselves and their interests, connecting with any comments they make, and continuing the conversation with related topics are easy ways to move the conversation from its initial surface into a more meaningful territory.

Share a little of your vulnerability during conversions to encourage others to open up. For example, "I'm not very confident when it comes to puzzle games." This will prompt them to share one or two of their own vulnerabilities, but be careful not to scare people away with too much negativity.

To avoid social anxiety disorder, gradually expose yourself to social gatherings. Practice talking to people slowly, even if only for a few seconds at a time, and after a while of exchanging greetings, it will turn into a short conversation.

Start a friendship even if you're not sure they'll like you.

Express your emotions both verbally and non-verbally without considering the consequences. Just start the conversation, as the worst that can happen is that the person ignores you.

Group conversations can encourage you to be expressive, though you may struggle to get their attention. Raise your hands or make a gesture to get their attention, then begin speaking.

Being curious during a conversation will help you stay focused and interested. Introverts can easily zone out or become distracted during a conversation, but if you're curious, you'll be on the lookout for what the other person will say next.

Hacks to Help Deepen Initial Connection

Be genuine and honest. Don't try to fool others to impress them because you'll lose that connection the moment they figure it out.

Work out what is appropriate and what is not in social interactions. It's important to keep things light-hearted and avoid topics that could put the relationship at risk.

Pay attention and nod while the other person is speaking, as they need to know you're paying attention to them.

Share information about yourself that is not visible on the surface. This will give your connection a unique air of exclusivity.

Be aware and present as you communicate. Demonstrate compassion and open-mindedness without drama. There will be disagreements, but don't be dramatic about it.

Do things that demonstrate to others that you truly love and care about them.

When listening to others, be empathic. Listen to understand rather than to respond.

Spend quality time with your friends to strengthen your bonds and make more memories.

During a conversation, making eye contact shows that you are confident and interested in the subject.

All of this is topped off with a smile. A smile brightens the moods of others and allows them to relax and feel at ease in your presence.

Speaking with strangers or people you know isn't as difficult as it seems if you use small talk to put them at ease. A good two-way conversation is when you can express yourself and learn about others. Small talk will be required to initiate conversation, whether you are an extrovert or an introvert, especially with strangers.

The deaf rely so heavily on body language for expression and communication, so avoid sending mixed messages with your gestures and actions. As you put all of these tips and guidelines into action, keep a journal of your experiences so you can learn from your experiences to help you do better in the future.

Chapter 6: Instantly Master the Art of Storytelling

Did you know that storytelling is one of the oldest forms of communication? It's true. For centuries, people have been using stories to communicate ideas, values, and principles because stories can move people in a way that other methods can't.

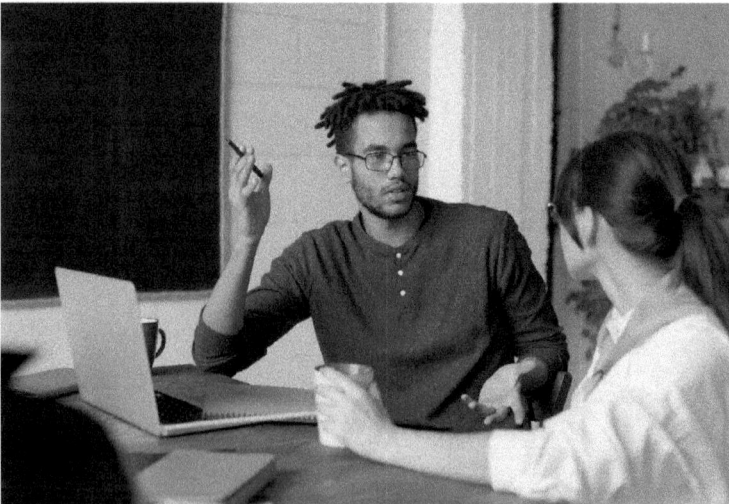

People have been using stories to communicate ideas, values, and principles for centuries.
https://www.pexels.com/photo/photo-of-man-holding-pen-3182752/

It's no surprise that storytelling is back in fashion again. Everywhere you look, there are examples of brands using this technique to promote their products. But you may wonder, "How do I tell a story?" And more importantly, "What does it mean to tell a story?" While not everyone is born with the innate ability to tell stories that keep people on the edge of their seats, there are a few methods to develop and improve this ability. This chapter will explain everything you need to know about confidently telling a story, so read on to discover how!

What Is Storytelling?

Storytelling is simply the act of sharing a story from your life. Whether it's a funny anecdote or a challenging experience, the goal of storytelling is to connect with others by sharing your life experiences. The simplest and most effective form of storytelling is a first-person narrative, which involves you taking the role of the main character instead of retelling a story as if you were a spectator. It is an ancient art form that can be applied to almost any situation, whether in the classroom, at an event, or in the boardroom. It's an effective tool because it allows you to connect with an audience on a personal level by revealing aspects of your personality and providing examples of how you've applied your values in life. At the same time, it also allows you to relate to others by exposing common struggles and providing useful insights that can be applied to a variety of situations.

The Power of Storytelling to Develop Communication Skills

Are you someone who avoids eye contact, fidgets in a meeting, or speaks mostly about yourself? Then you're missing out on opportunities to build stronger relationships at work and socially. There are many ways to develop as a person and grow—but difficult conversations, team-building exercises, and insincere job interviews don't have to be among them. In fact, they can often be counterproductive. That's why so many people feel trapped in their comfort zone. Shyness, fear of saying the wrong thing, or fear of being misunderstood are all common roadblocks when it comes to communicating more authentically. A personal growth program can help make you comfortable enough to speak up and be yourself in any setting. However, it can also be as simple as adding storytelling as part of your communication skills toolkit —and here's why.

Storytelling is a powerful tool for developing communication skills because it forces you to slow down, analyze your feelings, and then constructively articulate them. By sharing a story, you're exploring your own feelings and bringing up a variety of emotions that may not have been present had you simply stated a fact or objective. This process can help you develop a more empathetic and authentic communication style. Storytelling is also a great tool for building trust, as it lets you peel back the layers of your personality and show your true self to others. By doing so, you can help others feel more comfortable communicating with you, as they're able to get a better sense of who you are and how you might respond in various situations.

How to Use Storytelling to Improve Your Communication Skills

It's easy to incorporate storytelling into your day-to-day life. You can use it when you're speaking to a friend or colleague, giving feedback to a direct report, or leading a meeting.

Here are a few ways you can use storytelling to enhance your communication skills:

- **Start with yourself** - First and foremost, you should begin by telling stories about yourself. This is especially important in the workplace, as you'll likely find that many of your colleagues are also hesitant to speak up. By sharing stories about your mistakes and successes, you can open up the conversation so that others will feel comfortable sharing as well

- **Share stories about a group** - Once you've become more comfortable sharing stories about yourself, you can start sharing stories about your team at work or your group of friends or family. This can help others feel more connected and make it easier to have difficult conversations by showing empathy and building trust. It can also help you identify areas where you may need to provide more guidance or coaching

- **Share stories about your clients** - If you work in a business-to-business setting, you can also use storytelling to help your clients feel more comfortable communicating with your company. Try sharing stories about clients who have struggled with a particular issue and how your company has addressed the challenge. This will help your clients feel at ease when communicating with your team and give them useful real-life examples they can apply to their own situations.

Why Storytelling Is an Effective Communication Tool

Storytelling is an effective communication tool because it helps you demonstrate empathy. By sharing a story, you're connecting with others by showing them the situations you've been in where you've struggled or succeeded. This will help others to not feel like they're alone and gives them a good example of how to deal with a similar situation in the future. In a workplace setting, it's common for people to feel they're in competition with one another rather than working toward a common goal. This can block collaboration and make it more challenging to work together toward a mutual outcome. By sharing a story about a previous experience or challenge, you can help others feel less alone and give them a better understanding of the pressures you face. This can help people feel like they can rely on you more and create a more collaborative environment.

Different Storytelling Styles: What's Your Style?

Let's say you are planning to narrate a story. Which style should you adopt? How can you make the story more interesting? Or, how can you make it more appealing to your listeners? A story is something that has a narrative, characters, and setting. However, not all stories are the same. There are different types of stories, and you can choose the type of story you want to tell depending on the situation. You can also mix and match them to get the best results.

Tell a Story That Makes People Laugh

Most of the time, the audience will be in a group setting, like a work environment or a social event. You can tell this story when you want people to feel good and have a great time together. You can use humor as a way to deal with some situations and make them more enjoyable. You don't need to be too serious with this type of story. You can make it a bit funny too. You can also use your own personal experience or an incident you happened to come across to tell a funny story. You can choose to tell a funny story at a wedding or any other event where you want people to be happy. A funny story will make your guests laugh and help them enjoy the event even more.

Tell a Dramatic Story

There are different types of stories, but some are more dramatic than others. A dramatic story could be about a tragedy you came across or an incident where there were a lot of conflicts, such as during a war. Dramatic stories are often about the unfairness of life and how humans struggle to cope with it. If you want to tell a dramatic story, you should find something that is interesting and meaningful. You can also choose to tell a dramatic story to help someone struggling with a situation they are facing or raise awareness about an issue.

Tell an Informative Story

An informative story provides information related to a topic, such as science, history, or the news. If you are planning to tell an informative story, you need to do some research first. You need to know what information you want to share with your audience. You can also use your own personal experience to tell an informative story. You can tell the story of how you experienced a situation or what you learned from it. You can also tell the story of how you overcame a challenge in your life. An informative story is helpful when you want to share information with your audience or your classmates, or you can even tell it on the radio or when you are narrating a video. An informative story can hold your audience's attention and make them interested in the topic you are talking about.

How to Tell a Story: The Art of Communicating Your Message

People love a good story. They're how we learn about each other and the world around us. There's nothing more enjoyable than being transported to a new place, time, or experience through the exchange of stories. Nurturing your ability to tell a story will help you connect with others on a deeper level and potentially open doors for you in your career and personal life. If you can find the perfect balance between brevity and detail, an anecdote helps your audience see the world from a new perspective. And with the right framework and structure, your story will have a lasting impact on your audience. By breaking down these principles into simple steps, you'll find it easier to communicate effectively as an individual or team member in any situation.

Know Your Audience

This may seem obvious, but knowing who you're speaking to and how they prefer to be engaged will help you tailor your story for maximum effect.

- **Professional:** In a professional setting, you'll have a better chance of being heard if you keep your story short and to the point. This means using only the information relevant to your point and leaving the rest out. If you're speaking at a conference or giving a keynote speech, you won't have the same amount of time to tell a story as you would in a one-on-one conversation. So, you'll need to be more concise and cut out all unnecessary chatter.

- **Social:** If you're in a more casual setting, you'll have more freedom to expand on your story and really paint a picture for your audience. Just remember that you still have a goal with this story. If you don't have a purpose for sharing it, then don't bother.

Hook 'Em with an Opener

This is your chance to get the full attention of your audience. You've got their attention with the topic, but now you want to hold onto it. One way to do this is to set up a sort of "trap" for your audience. By creating an expectation in your audience with a short phrase, you can surprise them with the rest of your story. A great example of this is a story about a man who has a hard time getting his car out of the driveway in the winter. The storyteller begins by saying, "When winter hits, and it's time to put your car away, there's one thing you need to remember: Don't forget to shovel the snow off your car!"

Establish Context

An old Japanese proverb says, "If you don't know where you are, you don't know who you are." Before you dive into the heart of your story, you want to give your audience a little context about where it takes place. This means finding a way to introduce the characters you are talking about and the specific situation or environment in which your story takes place. For example, if you're telling a story about the last time you went on vacation, you might want to give some context about who was there and what the weather was like. This will help your audience to picture themselves in this situation.

Tell the Main Event

The core of your story is what happened. It's the moment when everything changes, and you or your character is forced to adapt to a new situation they found themselves in. There are a few key things to keep in mind as you dive into this portion of the story:

- **Find the right balance between brevity and detail**: This means that you don't want to get too bogged down by the specifics of the event. It's not a play-by-play recall of everything that happened.

- **Focus on the main character of the story:** Who was involved in the event? What role did they play? What is the character's relationship to your audience? You want to bring this character to life for your audience.

- **Take responsibility for the event:** Your main event should be presented as something that happened to you and not something that "just happened."

- **Use concrete details to paint a picture for your audience:** By using specific examples and details, you help your audience to fully immerse themselves in the story.

Wrap up with a Conclusion

This is where you take everything that happened in your story and apply it to the lesson you want your audience to walk away with. There are a few different ways to go about this. You can tie the story back to a specific person, idea, or feeling. Or, you can walk the audience through the steps you took to come out on top. Whatever you decide to do, your conclusion should feel like a natural extension of the story. You don't want to end up with a conclusion that feels abrupt or forced.

Keep these three things in mind when crafting your conclusion:

1. **Be clear:** You want your conclusion to be unmistakable. It can't be open to interpretation. It needs to be clear and direct.

2. **Be concise:** You don't want to ramble on and on until your audience starts to lose interest. Make your point and move on.

3. **Keep it positive:** While it's crucial to learn from your mistakes, your conclusion should be more about what you learned and less about the "wrong" things that happened.

Exercises for Better Storytelling

While you can't force everyone to listen, you can prepare yourself to share stories that elicit a particular reaction by practicing techniques that help you to feel more confident sharing stories.

Here are a few tips to help you become a better storyteller:

- **Choose a story that resonates with you** - The first thing you should do when preparing to share a story is to think about which stories resonate with you the most. This could be a challenging experience you've faced or an anecdote that makes you laugh. Once you've decided which story you'd like to share, ask yourself why it resonates with you. This will help you prepare for the conversation and make it easier for you to transition from the story back to the present.

- **Understand the story** - This doesn't mean you have to memorize the entire story, but you should try to understand the main point and how it applies to the conversation at hand. This will help you transition seamlessly from the story back to the present and provide others with a better understanding of what you're trying to say. Try keeping a journal and writing down anything out of the ordinary that happens to you or someone else. This will make your storytelling feel more realistic.

- **Connect with your audience** - Once you've shared the story, try to make eye contact with as many people in the room as possible. This will help you engage with your audience and show that you're connected with them and the story. This can also help you identify any questions or concerns that the audience may have so you can address them effectively.

Here are some tips to help you become more comfortable sharing stories:

- **Pick a few stories** - Before you jump into a conversation, try to think about the stories that you'd like to share. This helps you prepare for the conversation and makes it easier to transition from the story back to the present. You can try picking a few stories which address challenges your team is facing and how you're working to overcome them. Alternatively, you can search YouTube for comedians or podcasters and use their storytelling abilities as inspiration.

- **Prepare yourself** - Before you hop into the conversation, try to get yourself in the right mindset. This may mean taking a few deep breaths, meditating, or practicing a breathing exercise. Alternatively, you can try thinking about the examples you're going to share and how they apply to your team. This will help you stay focused during the conversation and keep you from getting overwhelmed by the attention.

- **Practice makes perfect** - Once you've committed to becoming a more confident storyteller, practice. This doesn't mean you have to memorize the story by heart, but you can try to get used to sharing it in conversations. The outcome will mean you are more comfortable speaking up, and this will make it easier for you to transition from the story back to the present.

Communicating your message effectively is an art form. It's not something that comes naturally to everyone, but it can be learned and improved with practice. If you're looking to become a better storyteller, try putting yourself in situations where you have to tell a story. Whether that's at a family gathering or in the office, you'll find that it's a great way to improve your communication skills. When all is said and done, a well-told story can capture any audience, be it with friends, over a beer, or with colleagues in a meeting. Just remember to know your audience, establish context, tell the main event, and wrap up with a conclusion, and you'll be well on your way to becoming a better storyteller.

Chapter 7: 15 Tips to Communicate in Groups Effortlessly

Communication is one of the most important skills you can have. It's also something that many people struggle with, especially in a group setting.

Communication is one of the most important skills you can have
https://www.pexels.com/photo/colleagues-shaking-each-other-s-hands-3184291/

When speaking with just one other person, we are able to clearly express our thoughts and get our message across. However, once there are more than two people involved, things get much trickier.

In group settings, it's easy to feel left out or overlooked when everyone else seems to be getting along so well. Because of this, being able to communicate effectively within a group setting is a very useful skill to have.

If you find yourself struggling with communication in group settings, read on for some helpful tips to change your social dynamic for the better!

Why Communicating within a Group Setting Can Be Difficult

When working in a large team or out with a group of friends, the ability to communicate clearly and effectively is crucial. Unfortunately, these are skills not everyone possesses. In any group environment, there is a risk that communication will be stifled by shyness, antagonism, or introversion. People have their own personalities and life experiences that can make communication difficult.

And let's face it – not everyone is great at making small talk. As much as we all love getting to know new people, most of us would prefer if group settings were a little less awkward. We all want to be that person who makes those around us feel comfortable and at ease. But when you're in a situation where you don't know anyone, it can be hard to break the ice. If you struggle with building rapport with new people, it's probably because you're not speaking their language or you don't understand theirs. Most people are more likely to open up and trust someone who has an interest in similar things or who understands their interests. Our ability to make friends and build rapport with those around us is directly related to our communication skills. Whether you're an introverted individual or simply someone who struggles to meet new people, learning the ins and outs of communication is part of feeling more confident and capable. With this in mind, here are some communication tips for group settings that will help you make friends and build rapport with everyone around you.

Prevent Others from Talking over You

It can be extremely frustrating if you're in a situation where people keep interrupting you. It is disrespectful and can make it difficult to feel comfortable and build a rapport with people. If you notice that people are interrupting you, there are some things you can do to stop this and prevent others from talking over you.

- First of all, try to make eye contact with the person who is interrupting you and give them a slight nod or a head tilt to let them know that you're ready for them to speak. This will help them realize that you've not finished talking yet.

- You can also use non-verbal cues to try and get the attention of the person who is interrupting you. Folding your arms, for example, can send a signal that you need to finish what you're saying.

Communicate Clearly

Communication is the transfer of information between people so that they can understand each other. The clearer you are in your conversation, the quicker and more effectively you will be able to convey your message, and the less chance there is of causing confusion or misunderstanding. You can increase clarity in your interaction by using simple language, making eye contact, and asking questions.

- Write down your ideas and thoughts before you communicate them. This helps you to organize your thoughts and choose the right words to express yourself effectively.

- Make sure you're looking directly at the person you're communicating with. This will show them that you're focused on what they're saying and that you're engaged and interested.

- Ask questions if you're not sure the person understands what you're saying. This will also show that you're engaged and interested in what they have to say.

Confirm Understanding

While you should also work to ensure that you fully understand the other person's message, it's also worth bearing in mind that you don't want to put words in someone else's mouth. To avoid this, you can use a few key phrases like "I think what you're trying to say is..." or "Does this mean...?" to confirm that you fully understand their message. This can help avoid misunderstandings between you and the other person and reinforce that you're actively listening. By confirming that you understand, you'll also make the other person feel more confident in your abilities as a communicator. This will also make you look more professional and capable, which will be beneficial in the long run.

Attract Attention

If you're in a group setting and want to get someone's attention, be aware of how you're doing it. By simply raising your hand, you may come across as aggressive, whereas by waving your hand, you're being more receptive.

- If you want to attract the attention of someone who is sitting across from you at a table, you can use the palm-up wave. This is considered a receptive gesture.

- If you want to attract the attention of someone who is sitting beside you, you can use the palm-down wave, which is considered more aggressive.

- Another way to attract attention in a group setting is by using non-verbal sounds. If you want to call attention from someone who is on your left, for example, you can use a "tsk" sound with your tongue to get their attention.

- Be opinionated. In a group, its members tend to direct their communicative attention more to people who have stronger opinions, as the article "Interpersonal communication in small groups" published in the Journal of Abnormal and Social Psychology shows.

Be Mindful of Body Language

Your body language can have a huge impact on your communication. If you're hunched over, crossing your arms, and avoiding eye contact, people will see you as closed-off and uninterested in what they have to say. While you should always be mindful of how you present yourself, it can be particularly useful when you're communicating with a large group of people. If the majority of your team sits at the back of the office and you sit at the front, it will send out a very different impression. Taking care of your body language will give off a much more confident and engaging impression and make communication much easier.

Communication Works Both Ways

Communication is a two-way street, and it's essential to ensure that you're actively listening to the other people in your group. While you should be mindful of the people speaking and actively listening, you should also be checking in with the rest of the group. This can help to avoid any one-on-one discussions getting out of hand or becoming distractions, but it can also help you avoid putting your foot in it. If you notice that a few people are looking frustrated or disengaged, you can use this as an opportunity to check in with the group as a whole. By actively checking in with the rest of the group, you can identify potential issues and repair any damaged relationships before they become serious problems.

Take Control

If you're new to the group or want to steer a conversation to a particular topic, ensuring you have control over the conversation can help you build rapport with others. If you have to take control of the conversation, doing so abruptly can be uncomfortable for other people and will make it harder to build rapport. Instead, try bridging into the topic with a question. Asking a question is a great way to steer a conversation and lead it to a particular topic that you want to discuss. If you're nervous about taking control of the conversation, you can start with a general question that everyone can contribute to.

Watch Your Vocabulary

You might be tempted to use big and impressive words to sound like you know what you're talking about. However, this can backfire and make you sound less intelligent. You should watch your vocabulary in a few different ways:

- Avoid using jargon or industry-specific language where possible. Unless you're talking to other members of your team or in a meeting, this can make you sound like you're trying to show off, and if used incorrectly, it makes you seem like a complete fool.

- Make sure that the words you use are appropriate for the person you're talking to. If they're not a scientist, don't talk to them like they are! This may sound obvious, but it can easily be overlooked.

- Avoid using words that may be considered offensive or using offensive phrases. You never know what other people's backgrounds and experiences are and the last thing you want to do is make someone feel uncomfortable or offend anyone.

Ask Questions and Be an Active Listener

Active listening will help you communicate better by building trust between you and the person you're speaking to, so you can understand where they're coming from. If you're speaking with someone and want to help them open up, asking questions is a great way to do so. You can use open-ended questions, which are questions that can't be answered with a yes or no. You can also ask them if they want to share a story. This can be helpful if the other person is someone you look up to or admire.

Eye Contact and Body Language

Did you know that communication happens more than verbally? In fact, non-verbal communication accounts for at least two-thirds of the communication process. When you're in a group setting, you want to focus on eye contact and other non-verbal cues as you normally would in one-on-one communication. Eye contact is sometimes seen as intimidating when you're speaking to one other person, but it's important in a group setting because it helps you connect with others and build rapport with them. When communicating with others, you want to be aware of a handful of things. Your posture says a lot about you, and you want to make sure that it's open and inviting. You also want to ensure you're not blocking anyone from the conversation or actively forcing them to look away from you. Be aware of your hands and make sure that they're not blocking someone out or that they are being used aggressively.

Use Small Talk

Small talk is simply the casual and informal exchange of superficial remarks. When you're in a new group setting, the best way to begin is by asking questions related to the event or the surroundings.

- If you're at a networking event, you may ask who some people are and what they do.
- If you're at a wedding, you may ask who is married to whom and how long they've been together.

- At a conference or lecture, you could ask what the speakers are most excited about and what people are excited about in the industry.

- You can also ask about the group and if anyone knows each other.

- You want to be sure to ask open-ended questions. These types of questions invite deeper and more interesting responses from the group. Closed-ended questions are more likely to result in short, surface-level answers and no further conversation.

Tell Stories

Stories are one of the most effective ways to create a connection with those around you. There are many types of stories that you can tell in a group setting to help you build a connection.

- If you're at a wedding and know that the bride is a huge sports fan, instead of asking about her career, you could ask about her favorite sports team, and then you could share a story about one of your favorite games and teams.

- If you're at a networking event and know that the person you're talking to is hoping to get a promotion soon, instead of asking about the company or their job, you could ask about their career, and then you could share a story about your experience with promotions and the best ways to earn them.

Establish Commonalities

If you've been talking with a group of people for a while and have established some rapport, you can try to discover commonalities that exist between you and the group. The goal here is to discover what people are most passionate about in their lives and work. People tend to be more engaged and excited when talking about the things they enjoy.

Use Humor

Humor is a great way to break the ice and make a lasting connection with the people around you. If you're unsure about making small talk and breaking the ice with a group, try using humor to help you get started. You can try to bring humor into your questions or stories or use it in a self-deprecating way. Self-deprecation involves making light of your own flaws and mistakes in a self-aware way that is meant to make you less serious and less intimidating. You may notice that the people around you are hesitant to speak up or ask questions. If this is the case, using humor can help you break the ice and encourage everyone to feel more comfortable speaking up.

Share Things about Yourself

This is a great tip to remember when building rapport with almost any group. People want to know if you've done things in your life that you're proud of. Share your achievements and the other things in your life that you're proudest of. You might be at a wedding and be proud of graduating from university or getting a promotion at work. You may be at a networking event and be proud of starting your own business or receiving an award for your work. Depending on the group, you may also want to share your passions and interests. You can do this by mentioning what you're most excited about in your life, and be sure to mention the things that you've achieved.

Practical Exercises

To help you get started with group communication, here are the essential components you need to work on the next time you find yourself in a group setting.

Make Yourself Heard

Instead of letting feelings build up inside, be the one to speak up and express what you're feeling.

Another advantage of speaking up is that it allows other people to speak up too. By listening attentively and respectfully, everyone can feel included in the conversation. Nobody should feel as though they're being left out. By speaking up, you are doing your part to create a positive environment for everyone to feel comfortable enough to share their feelings. Speaking up also creates a sense of accountability, which helps keep people on track with their goals and keeps them accountable to each other.

Finally, speaking up helps to show that you respect yourself. How can you expect others to do so if you don't value your own thoughts and feelings? By speaking up and expressing yourself, you demonstrate that you respect yourself enough to listen to what you have to say. So, make sure that you acknowledge people as they speak, ask questions when appropriate, and listen carefully to what others are saying.

Be Prepared for Different Answers

One of the biggest challenges for anyone is knowing how to get the most out of it. How do you know what is going on? What should you be looking for? How can you best contribute to the discussion? One of the keys to successfully navigating a group discussion is to be prepared. This means being ready to respond when asked questions or making comments of your own. In addition: Be aware that different people will have different perceptions. Don't be afraid to disagree with someone's opinion or diverge from the group consensus if you feel strongly about it. But don't get too far off track by trying to argue against everyone else, either. Remember that people are allowed to have their own opinions as long as they are respectful and considerate when expressing them.

Empathize

Empathy is the ability to understand and share another person's feelings. Empathetic listening means taking a moment to put yourself in someone else's shoes. For example, imagine how it feels to be frustrated by a long commute or how scary it must be to have cancer. Empathetic listening is especially necessary when you're talking with people who may be experiencing difficult emotions. It can help you recognize their needs and show that you care about them.

There are many ways to listen with empathy:

- **Listen actively.** Avoid distractions like checking your phone or multitasking. Instead, focus on what the other person is saying and try to understand where they're coming from.

- **Be open-minded and nonjudgmental.** Don't assume that people will automatically agree with your point of view, but don't ignore their opinions either — take them into account when making your own decisions.

- **Show empathy through your tone of voice.** Speak clearly and calmly without getting defensive or sarcastic. If you find yourself becoming frustrated, try pausing before answering or try another approach (such as asking questions or paraphrasing).

Communication is not just about saying the words that come out of your mouth. It is an entire process that includes how you behave, make eye contact, and tone of your voice. If you want to make friends and build a rapport with people in a group setting, communicate using eye contact and body language. Use small talk to learn about the group and the things they are interested in. Tell stories, discover commonalities, and finally, be confident and proud of yourself and your achievements. Most importantly, be yourself and remember that building rapport is about being comfortable with people, so don't try too hard to be something you're not.

Chapter 8: Become an Amazing Public Speaker

Public speaking is a skill that many people fear and do everything they can to avoid. This fear can often inhibit the career prospects of even the most talented individuals. The National Institutes of Mental Health found that 75 percent of people fear public speaking. Some people fear it because of how many different audiences they may address (e.g., large groups). Others are terrified by the thought of giving a speech or talking to a single person who wields power over them, such as their supervisor, interviewer, and professor, during an oral exam.

Public speaking is a skill that many people fear and do everything they can to avoid.
https://www.pexels.com/photo/man-beside-flat-screen-television-with-photos-background-716276/

Public speaking can be a challenging undertaking. Nervousness is a part of life, and being nervous about public speaking is no exception. Some people are naturally gifted speakers and can command an audience with ease. For those who aren't, it takes time, practice, and patience to improve their skills. Public speaking is like riding a bike. You can only do it if you get on and start pedaling. You may be surprised at how much easier it is to speak in front of people when you know what to expect.

The following is a guide to help you understand the process of public speaking and how to overcome your fears. It's vital that you approach the task with an open mind and leave any preconceived ideas behind. There is no right or wrong way to do it as long as you are honest with yourself and your audience.

Lack of Confidence

You'll risk alienating the audience if you don't have confidence in yourself and the topic you're talking about. A confident speaker connects with the audience and makes them feel like they're part of the discussion. If you're not confident, it will show in your body language and the way you speak. You may struggle to make eye contact with your audience or struggle to stay on topic. You may also be tempted to use filler words like "um" and "ah," making it sound like you're not sure of what you're saying. To build self-confidence in public speaking, you should identify and address what causes your lack of confidence. Here are some of the common causes:

Preparation

A good public speaker is always prepared. Even if you're not a naturally confident person, you can still build self-confidence as a public speaker by preparing yourself adequately. Come up with an outline of what you want to say, and practice it several times before giving your speech. This will help you avoid making mistakes or forgetting what comes next in your presentation. You should also practice reading your speech aloud. This will help you get used to speaking in front of an audience, which is a key part of building self-confidence as a public speaker.

Visualization

Visualization is a technique that helps you get comfortable with the idea of public speaking. To use it, imagine yourself giving your speech and seeing yourself succeed. Try to picture as many details as possible. How are people responding? Are they laughing at your jokes? Can you see them nodding their heads in agreement? Imagine every aspect of the situation, including how you feel while delivering the speech. This will help you get used to what it will be like when you actually give the presentation.

Self-Talk

A lot of people have negative thoughts about public speaking. These can include things like "I'm going to mess up" or "Everyone will think I'm stupid for saying this." If you have these thoughts, try replacing them with more positive ones. Replace the thought "I'm going to mess up" with "No one will notice if I make a mistake. It happens all the time at presentations, and no one minds." This technique is called self-talk because it involves talking yourself through the situation using positive affirmations instead of negative statements.

Confidence follows action. The more you try something and succeed, the more confident you will be in that particular skill. For example, playing a musical instrument. At first, your fingers fumble, and you're embarrassed to make mistakes in front of others—but with practice, you grow more confident and soon learn how to play well enough so that other people enjoy listening. To become confident as a speaker, it is essential that you practice regularly in front of other people. Practice in front of a mirror or on video. You need to be able to see yourself speaking so that you can notice when you are making mistakes and learn from them.

Lack of Attention to the Audience

To be a successful public speaker, you need to know your audience. Maybe you are aware that some members of your audience might be hostile to or skeptical about what you're proposing. You may be confident in your ability as a speaker but worry that your audience may not relate to you. You can eliminate the disconnection by identifying the gaps and tackling them accordingly.

For example, if you are speaking about a new type of software for business owners and your audience includes executives who are not technically adept, it may be helpful to provide more details than you would otherwise. If your talk is aimed at entrepreneurs, but some of your audience members work in large companies that aren't likely to use the product you're promoting, they may appreciate hearing how they can help their firms benefit from what you're proposing. While you can't always predict what your audience will need, you should at least make an effort to account for it. The following are some tips to help you identify the needs of your listeners:

Research the Audience

You've probably heard the old adage that "a little knowledge is a dangerous thing," and it's especially true when you're speaking. Researching your audience can help you tailor your talk so it meets their needs rather than simply pushing your own agenda. It also gives you a chance to make sure that whatever point of view you have on a subject does line up with theirs. If there are any major differences between what they think and what you do, those differences should be addressed during the presentation rather than just ignored. One of the best ways to research your audience is through surveys. Surveys can be as simple as an email or paper survey you send out before an event, or they can be more elaborate and include a website where people can post comments about their ideas on a subject. When preparing to speak at an event, consider what your audience might want and need from the talk.

Researching your audience beforehand will help you to engage with them more personally and make your speech more interesting. You should also try to understand what motivates your audience. If you can figure out what drives them, finding common ground with them and speaking a language they understand will be easier.

Hook Your Audience Fast

The hook is the first thing you say or do to grab your audience's attention. It should be a simple statement that makes an immediate connection with your audience and shows them what they can expect from you during the speech. The hook should also be brief, memorable, and relevant to your audience. You can use a rhetorical question, quote a well-known person or authority on the subject, or tell a quick anecdote that illustrates what you'll be discussing in more detail later.

Tell a Compelling Story

One of the most effective ways to make your audience listen is by telling a compelling story as you have read previously. It doesn't have to be an elaborate story full of plot twists and turns, but it should be an interesting and engaging one that makes your audience want to hear more. A great story can be used as a hook to get the audience's attention or woven throughout your speech. You can also use it to illustrate a point or reinforce an idea.

Lack of Preparedness

Before giving a speech, practice it in its entirety. Doing so allows you to hear where you are rushing or mumbling words and also allows your voice intonation and enthusiasm levels to feel natural. Using visuals, technology, or other aids beforehand also makes it possible to catch and eliminate glitches in the presentation. Rehearsal prepares speakers to be more familiar with their material so they can field questions effectively. Your speech will be filled with stumbles and awkward pauses when you don't practice. You may lose your place in the text and need to turn pages or notes. The audience will see that you are nervous and uncomfortable, which doesn't inspire confidence in your message. To be better prepared before the speech, you should do the following:

Gather Early Feedback

The best way to prepare for your speech is to talk about it with others. They can provide feedback on your presentation's content, delivery, and style. Ask them if they understand what you are trying to communicate and whether anything is confusing or missing from your message. You should also ask them if they think the speech is interesting and whether it will hold the audience's attention. Ask them how they would improve or change your presentation. You may need to rewrite some parts or add details to keep people engaged and interested in what you are saying.

Use Your Voice and Body Language

Your voice and body language are two of the most powerful tools in your arsenal as a speaker. Use them to convey passion, enthusiasm, and emotion. Use the tone of your voice to emphasize important points and create excitement in your speech. A low or monotone voice can make you sound boring and uninterested in what you're saying. A high-pitched voice may make you sound too emotional – *as if every word is a big deal.* Find a happy medium where your voice has energy but doesn't go up and down like an elevator, as this will help keep your audience engaged.

Use body language to project confidence and authority even if you feel nervous or unsure. Stand up straight, smile, look at the audience while speaking, gesture with open palms when appropriate, and avoid fidgeting with things such as pens or papers on the podium. In one study, students who sat upright—as opposed to slouching—exuded more confidence and felt more confident about themselves. Walking confidently will let the audience know you have something valuable to share in your presentation. Use gestures to emphasize important points and create excitement in your speech.

For instance, you can use your hands to emphasize a point or gesture toward something in the audience. If you're talking about a new product available on your company's website, point to the URL on an overhead projector so people can see it. This will make them feel as though they can relate to and engage with the topic.

Listen to Yourself When You Speak

It may sound silly, but it's easy to get lost in your words and not hear yourself. While practicing, listen for awkward pauses or sounds that don't flow well with the rest of your sentence. If someone makes a comment during your speech, listen to the tone of their voice and how they phrase what they say. This will help you understand how others are receiving what you have to say just as much as it helps them understand you!

Lack of Time Management

Always run through the speech before you deliver it. This is how you iron out any kinks in the wording, and it gives you time to practice reading at the right speed. Speakers often run overtime because they aren't adequately prepared and can't get through their material in the allotted time. If you tend to run late, set the alarm on your watch or phone to go off five minutes before the end of your talk. Make sure it's in your pocket and set to silent mode. The vibrations will let you know when it's time to wrap things up. A good rule of thumb is to practice concluding your speech two minutes before the timer goes off. This gives you the time to catch up if you're slacking off or an audience member asks a question.

Overcoming Stage Fright

Stage fright can be a very uncomfortable experience. It can take over your thoughts, making it hard for you to concentrate on anything else. It can also affect your body and make you feel sick or tense. As well as being a very unpleasant experience, it can also be very damaging to your performance. Stage fright can be tough to overcome, but there are some things you can do.

Get in the Right Mindset

The first thing you need to do is get into the right mindset. Don't think of stage fright as an illness but rather as a normal human response. You're not alone in having these feelings, and it's okay for them to happen. They are very common feelings to performers. The more you think of stage fright as a normal response, the easier it will be to manage. Try not to think of yourself as a performer and instead just be in the moment. This can help you get over any feelings of anxiety or fear.

Try writing down your thoughts and feelings before you go on stage, so you have time to process them. You may find that your thoughts and feelings aren't as bad as you thought.

Belly Breathe

Belly Breathing is a great way to calm your nerves. It's a technique that will help you slow down and focus on the present moment, which can help prevent any feelings of anxiety or fear from taking over. To do this exercise:

1. Take a deep breath through your nostrils and let it out through your mouth.
2. Repeat this process three times.
3. Once you've completed three rounds of belly breathing, take a moment to focus on how your body feels. You may find that it's easier to relax and focus on the task at hand.

Greet Your Audience and Smile

The hardest part is to initiate the speech —and that's why you should start by greeting your audience. It's a simple but effective way to start the speech off on the right footing and can help put you at ease. When you enter the room, smile and look out at everyone in your audience, take a moment to think about what they want from this presentation, as it can make all the difference when it comes time to deliver your message.

Turn the Spotlight Around

When you're in a spotlight—whether that spotlight is bright, dim, or just flickering on and off—it can make you feel as though everyone else sees more of your flaws than they do when you're not on stage. So turn the attention around. Now it's on others rather than yourself. You can ask questions that involve the audience or share stories they can relate to. If you're giving a presentation on building a kitchen island, ask people what kind of island they would like to see in their home. That way, you'll turn the spotlight onto them and allow them to share their thoughts and ideas with one another—and with you.

Move!

If you're feeling nervous, it's easy to get locked into one position: standing in front of the audience, behind your podium. Movement helps to keep you focused and breaks up the monotony of standing still. Try moving around the stage periodically as you speak; this will give your audience a chance to see different angles and perspectives on what you're saying. If you're too nervous about moving on your own, try moving when someone in the audience asks a question or makes a comment. This can effectively keep the interaction going without having to come up with something new to say.

Pause Occasionally

Pausing occasionally while talking lets your audience digest what they have just heard – and provides an opportunity for them to ask questions. It will also give you a chance to catch your breath, which can be particularly handy if you're feeling nervous and need to take a moment before continuing. The best time to pause is after making a major point or when you've said something particularly important. Make sure you look at the audience while pausing, as this will help them follow what you're saying.

Picture the Audience Naked

One of the oldest tricks to overcome stage fright is to picture the audience naked. This will make them seem less intimidating and more approachable. This technique takes the pressure off you and puts it on the audience. You'll realize they can't be too critical or judgmental about what you say if they're naked. They'll just be people like everyone else! If you can't picture the audience naked, try imagining that they're wearing unflattering costumes. Maybe they're dressed as clowns or superheroes, or maybe their clothes are on backward. This will help you see them in a new light and make them less intimidating.

Public Speaking Exercises

Vocal Warmups

Vocal warmups are often associated with musicians, but they can help public speakers too. These exercises help ease tension and warm up your voice, so it's ready for public speaking. Try these vocal warmups before you get on stage:

- Humming
- Singing scales (for singers)
- Repeating vowel sounds to loosen your facial muscles

Although most public speakers do not need to hit particular notes while speaking, it is still a good idea for them to warm up.

Talking to the Mirror

One of the most effective public speaking practices is talking to a mirror. This can be done in front of a full-length mirror – or one positioned at an angle so that you can look at yourself from your audience's perspective. The point of this exercise is to look at yourself while speaking and see if you are making any physical movements that may distract your audience. If you are making gestures with your hands, try to keep them subtle by making smaller movements or only using one hand at a time. You can also practice smiling in the mirror so that you know how it will look when you are presenting.

Try Eliminating the Fillers

Filler words are "um" and "ah"—words that don't add value to what you're saying. Try this exercise to eliminate filler words from your speech patterns. Speak for as long as you can without using any of these words. If you find yourself using them, stop and start again.

Pick up an Object and Talk about It

This technique will help you to feel more comfortable talking about unfamiliar topics or improvising on the spot. Set up a timer for five minutes, pick a random object and talk about it. You'll find it surprisingly difficult. However, it will become second nature with practice. Combine it with the "Try Eliminating the Fillers" exercise for better results. This exercise comes in handy when dealing with the numerous unknown variables on-stage, like an audience member asking a question you don't know the answer to or the slides suddenly going blank.

Chapter 9: How to Manage an Argument Like a Boss

Arguments are a part of any relationship, whether it be romantic, platonic, or strictly professional. As long as we aren't clones of each other, there are always going to be misunderstandings and disagreements between different people. Arguments are impossible to prevent altogether, but we can navigate through them productively and gracefully.

Arguments are a part of any relationship, whether it be romantic, platonic, or strictly professional.

It's difficult to deal with conflict and resolve it peacefully, but it's also an incredibly valuable skill. Whether volatile, destructive emotions cloud your judgment or you're non-confrontational to the extreme, know that arguments don't have to be so stressful to handle. An argument is an opportunity to understand another person and strengthen your bond as a result.

Learning how to have a productive argument is a matter of practice, but first, you need to learn what that looks like. We don't get many examples of what a healthy argument looks like in our lives, but it is possible for you to make it the norm for your relationships. As you read on, actively reflect on your own behavior and how you can better your conflict resolution skills.

Understanding What Happens During an Argument

The words exchanged during an argument only scratch the surface of what's going on. There's an underlying structure to all verbal disagreements. We don't tend to notice it when we're in the heat of the moment, so see how these elements can be applied to arguments you've had. Here's a concrete example.

Charlotte is Emma's younger sister, and they live together in Emma's apartment. One day when she was out of the city due to work, Emma called Charlotte and told her to clean up the apartment. "I'll be receiving a very important client at our place, so it absolutely has to be spotless. They're a difficult person to please and kind of a germaphobe. I'm very stressed about this, so please make it presentable."

Charlotte had several tests to study for, but she postponed her studying to help her sister out. She then pulled an all-nighter to catch up with her studies. After Emma received her client, she went to Charlotte's room and told her, "I can't believe you would do this to me, Charlotte! When I came home, the TV was still dusty, and the client complained about it to me. I was so embarrassed! I know you had other things to do, but my job is what pays for our apartment."

Charlotte was quick to defend herself, "That just sounds like they were looking for things to be upset about! I did forget to wipe the TV clean, but everything else was spotless, wasn't it?"

But Emma wouldn't have any of it. "I don't know why it's so difficult for you to accept when you're wrong. You messed up, and there's nothing to really argue about. I don't even know if taking you was the right choice now."

Feeling defeated and not wanting to upset her sister any further, Charlotte just apologized and left. This argument was completely unproductive, and it put a strain on the sisters' relationship for weeks afterward. To really understand what happened here, we'll look at each argument as if it was made up of smaller arguments.

What Really Happened?

Most arguments break out because the involved parties disagree on what happened. Whose story is right? Was it really Charlotte's job to deep-clean the entire apartment? Was Emma throwing her weight around as the breadwinner to intimidate her sister? Whose responsibility is the upkeep of the apartment?

The Objective Truth; Who's Right?

During arguments, people get too hung up on who's "objectively correct" and immediately jump to try to convince the other party that they're right. Arguments aren't really about facts. Both Charlotte and Emma agreed that the TV was dusty. What they didn't agree on was whether it was such a big deal. Arguments are about conflicting perceptions, and there's no clear-cut "right or wrong" judgment we can pass on those.

What to Do About It

Free yourself from the impossible task of determining who's really in the right. Even if you could, that's not what the argument is about. When you're confronted with the need to make this judgment, think about the true facts and whether you disagree with the facts or your perception of them.

Refrain from stating your feelings and perception as "the truth." They may be your truth, but they're not a universal truth. Each party brings its own perceptions to the table. You most likely have a lot to learn from the other person, and they have a lot to learn from you too. Focus on looking at the argument from the other person's point of view and try to understand how they saw it.

Intent; Why Did They Say That?

A person's intentions greatly influence what we think about them, despite the final result of their actions. Whether or not someone thinks badly of you will also influence how an argument with them will go. Did Charlotte not give enough importance to Emma's plea? Did Emma mention that she was unsure of her decision to take Charlotte in because she wanted to subtly threaten her, to make a point, or did she just say that in the heat of the moment?

The number one mistake we make here is that we assume we know what someone's intentions are. In fact, we can't know. As humans, we have to do this to some extent, but it's gone too far when someone's imaginary intent is derailing an entire conversation.

People may act with good intentions yet still cause irreparable damage. They may act with mixed intentions for reasons unknown even to them. They may have bad intentions that we're unaware of. According to a study, intentions explain about 28% of the variance in future behavior.

What to Do About It

Be aware that you can't know what's going through the other person's head. People show their intentions through actions, but what may be clear and obvious to you may be total conjecture to someone else.

Rather than intent, focus on impact. Find out how your words impacted the other person, and let them know how their words impacted you. Ask them what they were thinking at that moment and whether their impact lined up with what they really meant to say.

The Blame Game; Whose Fault Is It?

Nobody likes to be burdened with blame. People will go to great lengths to not be burdened with blame, putting a lot more on the line than you'd think. Nobody likes to blame, not only because it doesn't feel good but also because they don't feel it's all their fault. The truth is that it really isn't.

Charlotte thought that she was asked to drop everything to help Emma on short notice, and she did her part, so she's not to blame. Emma thought that since Charlotte took on the responsibility of cleaning the apartment, she was to blame if it wasn't done perfectly.

As a third party, it's easy to see how each girl contributed to the problem. When we're participants, emotions run high, and it's not easy to admit mistakes. Talking about blame is not only useless, but it's a surefire way to anger the other party even more.

What to Do About It

When you think in "It's them or me" terms, you miss the bigger picture. It's not all your fault, and it's not all their fault. Instead of trying to get the "guilty" party to admit blame, understand that the argument took place between two people. Both of you contributed to it in different ways.

What Do I Do with All These Feelings?

Feelings are always messy. Unfortunately, arguments between people are almost always about feelings. When feelings come up in an argument, people almost always shy away from them because feelings cloud your objective judgment.

Openly showing your feelings can lead people to believe that you're too emotional or that you're too sensitive. For many of us, wearing your heart on your sleeve is risky. When you've been burned before, openly showing your vulnerabilities like we ought to show our feelings feels silly.

What if you get brushed off? What if your feelings hurt someone that you didn't intend to hurt? And are we ready to face what the other person feels about us? This is why people are wary of getting into the feeling's territory during arguments.

As messy as feelings are, you have to dive into them if you want to solve a nasty argument. "I'm very stressed about this, so please make it presentable" shows Emma's anxiety, frustration, and restlessness. "That just sounds like they were looking for things to be upset about," shows Charlotte's disbelief, hurt, and annoyance. These feelings were the crux of the argument, yet they were never discussed.

If you're someone who gets carried away by feelings of anger and hurt during an argument, bombarding the other person with them is also not the solution. Despite what the other person might have done to provoke you, your feelings are your responsibility. It's not right to unfairly barrage someone with your feelings, no matter what.

What to Do About It

First of all, you don't have to react to the first thing you feel. If your immediate reaction to someone's words is anger, you don't have to show it straight away. Take a few seconds to reflect and debate whether it'll steer the conversation in the right direction if you react with anger.

Before determining what you'll be doing in the future or how you'll be fixing the problem, there should be a conversation about feelings. Express yourself calmly and rationally, and let the other person express their feelings. Listen without judgment, and acknowledge that their feelings are as real as yours.

What Does This Say about Who I Am?

As we argue with someone else on the outside, we're having our own little argument on the inside too. Arguing with someone, especially someone we hold in high regard or care for, can drastically affect our self-esteem. Whether you "lose" or "win," an argument might also affect your self-image.

Charlotte's image as a helpful younger sister who earns her keep in the apartment is at stake. Emma's image as a stern but just older sister who provides for her family without being taken advantage of is at stake. What if the other party has good reasons to think you're not what you present yourself as? Your self-image is really what's at stake for you.

What to Do About It

Understand that this all-or-nothing thinking (I'm helpful or useless, I'm stern or a pushover) is wrong. It doesn't apply here. Build a more complex image of yourself. Sometimes, you'll have to act "out of character." That's okay because you aren't a character in a play but a complex human being.

As you realize this about yourself, understand that the same thing applies to the other person. Hold firm in who you believe yourself to be, but don't panic if you must let go for a moment.

What If I Don't Want to Argue?

The first question that needs to be answered as a potential argument rears its head is *whether it's even worth it to engage*. Indeed, you don't have to waste energy on every disagreement, but being non-confrontational and a people-pleaser to the extreme is incredibly unhealthy.

If someone or something is bothering you, and you keep arguing with yourself about whether to bring it up, you probably should. You keep going back and forth because, deep down, you know that standing down means you'll get taken for granted. Your feelings of insecurity will be left to fester, and the person you're mad at doesn't even have the chance to fix anything.

On the other hand, if you engage in an existing argument or start a new one, it may exacerbate the problem. The other party may get even more upset, and both of your feelings could get hurt despite anyone's intentions. It could even cause irreparable damage to the relationship between the two of you.

Engaging in an argument shouldn't be this nerve-wracking. Confrontation is always going to be challenging, and uncomfortable feelings will always be involved, but you can't expect to get better at it with no practice. When there's an issue, speak up. It's not worth keeping the peace with short-term tactics for a crumbling relationship anyway.

What's Really Holding You Back?

Not confronting a problem doesn't make it go away, so there are other things that make us default to non-confrontation. Confronting someone is dangerous, so we've withheld permission to argue from ourselves. Silence is safe, except not really. Analyze what you're saying to yourself when you assert that arguing is always bad.

I Don't Like Arguing

Most people don't. But you must argue if respect is being taken away from you, you're being ignored, or your voice is actively stifled. You have to take a stand because it's a healthy thing to do.

I'm Scared of Alienating Those I Argue With

Fear is a supremely useful emotion. It means that you're looking out for yourself and your loved ones. It's very unlikely that you'll alienate your loved ones with one argument, and much more likely that you already are by not giving them a chance to do right by you. Embrace your fear, and face it.

I'm Not Good at Making My Point

You argue from your own authority, and that's enough. As much as an argument feels like a battle zone, it's not. So why feel the need to make your point perfectly? You also won't get any good without practice, so make your point and be satisfied with it.

Arguments Are All about Winning, Which I Don't Like

"Winning" an argument can look different for everyone, though it usually means getting what you want. At the end of the day, we use arguments to enact a change, and winning an argument means the change we want will take place. At the end of a productive argument, your perception of "winning" may have changed to a "win" being meeting the other person in the middle.

How Can I Argue with Someone Who Has Power over Me?

The first thing to understand about power is that it's imaginary. Someone's power over you is whatever you imagine that power to be. This is just one more mental obstacle you're imposing on yourself.

You may think like this when you have to confront your boss or parent about something, but every boss needs workers, and every parent needs children to be who they are. All power originates from within us.

When I'm Honest and Truthful, I'm Not Taken Seriously

Being honest and showing your true feelings always builds your credibility. As previously mentioned, feelings are the crux of all arguments. Hiding your true feelings means you're actively working against yourself. If you're honest about your feelings, maybe you're not believed because of some other mistake you've made subconsciously.

In My Experience, Telling the Truth Is Dangerous

This isn't an axiom that's applicable to every argument. If you feel this way, it's more indicative of your relationships than a universal truth. Telling the truth shouldn't be dangerous. Analyze if you truly are in any real danger for telling the truth or if you're making that judgment due to having been burned in the past.

We Always Yell, and Nobody Wins in the End

There's usually very little listening if there's a lot of yelling. If you begin to listen, you're already starting to win. There are always other vulnerable emotions hidden just under anger or judgment. What pain drives this argument? Listen, and ask questions. The time for you to tell your side of the story is not when insults are being hurled at you.

What If I'm up against a Wall of Prejudice?

Although we all have prejudices, certain preconceived notions may be set in stone for some people. As you realize this, you feel as if you're arguing with a brick wall. If you feel as if nothing you're saying is getting through, your "win" may just be taking this experience with you and retreating.

Prejudice is built by self-interest, and reasoning doesn't work against self-interest. What may work is having the other person believe that you, too, are arguing in their best interest. Otherwise, be aware of someone's prejudices, and make a tactical retreat. If reason trumped all, we wouldn't have any prejudices in the first place.

How Do I Even Begin to Formulate an Argument?

You don't have to take out a pen and paper to formulate an argument. When an argument is in progress, that's out of the question anyway. If you're at a loss for words, try to structure your argument like a story.

Humans are predisposed to listen to stories. In fact, world memory champions are able to remember an astounding number of unrelated sequences and facts just by constructing stories around them. As people, we really like stories, so structure your argument like one.

If you want to bring attention to the consequences, start from the end. Otherwise, it's never a bad idea to start a story from the beginning.

When to Throw in the Towel? What We Can and Can't Change

Trying to engage in every argument is both emotionally and mentally exhausting. As you encounter more and more arguments, you'll realize that some of them are difficult beyond their rewards. The other person may be purposefully acting to annoy or get a rise out of us, their prejudices are too much to deal with, or they're completely unwilling to display their true feelings for you to see.

You can control your own reaction to this information, but you can't control anything the other party says or does. Where you draw your own boundaries depends on what you're comfortable with. In the beginning, this may be earlier than you'd like. Be realistic. Some discomfort is to be expected, but short-term solutions are okay to use for arguments that don't seem to have an end.

In a healthy argument, you're both on the same team. Listen, share your feelings, and always stay curious about what the other person is experiencing from their point of view.

Chapter 10: 23 Strategies to End a Conversation Smoothly

Conversations can happen anywhere—at an event, at a shop, while driving, on the phone, over a video call, etc. Along with starting a conversation, it's crucial to always have a strong exit plan which doesn't leave the impression that you're in a hurry, can't be bothered anymore, or are just disinterested. Ending a conversation is as crucial as starting one.

Conversations can happen anywhere—at an event, at a shop, while driving, or on the phone.
https://www.pexels.com/photo/photo-of-men-having-conversation-935949/

When you start a conversation positively and end it abruptly, you could undo all of your previous work and put the other person in a negative mood. Try to end conversations well to leave a positive impression and increase your chances of speaking with the person again. Each conversation you have will end differently, so familiarize yourself with all of your options beforehand.

Make a lasting impression people will remember when you end a conversation and make a good first impression. Sometimes conversations can become awkward, so knowing how to leave a situation is a useful skill to have. You should gracefully end it as soon as you've determined whether the conversation has reached its elastic limit.

When you realize you're bored, it's better to stop talking. Sometimes, you end up saying things that are out of place or start repeating yourself when you run out of things to say. When an interaction reaches its peak and starts to wane, leave to end it professionally. This will make people want more of your time as a result. Instead of waiting for things to get awkward, you should end it with a sense of excitement.

What Causes an Awkward End to a Conversation?

When a conversation slows down to the point where each person is only speaking once every 30 seconds, it is likely coming to an end. It doesn't feel right when it gets to the point where there is nothing else to say, and one of you physically separates from the other out of boredom.

It's a warning sign that the conversation won't go well when you're unsure of how to end it but are frantically trying to think of something to say until someone else steps in. Making a big impact right away and then waiting until the energy is almost gone is not a good way to end a conversation. Whether or not it started out well, it should end well. Being glad that a conversation has ended indicates it did not go well. When there is no excitement – and there is also bad body language – conversations are difficult.

How to End a Conversation on a Good Note

If you had a positive impact on the other person during your interaction, make an effort to keep the momentum by making a strong exit. You have one more chance to affect how the conversation feels at its end. You did well if the interactions produced only positive feelings. Have a plan for how you want the conversation to end, such as "It was nice talking to you, hope to see you again," or "I'm glad we met, or "I'm looking forward to more meetings like this, but now I need to take care of something." Without a solid exit strategy, it would be impossible to leave a positive impression.

Conversation-Ending Strategies for Various Situations

In casual or cooperative conversations, consider the following options for exiting, which will make the other person remember you positively. Whether you're talking to a friend or an acquaintance, at a social gathering such as a party, or to a stranger on the road, you can use any of these options to end your conversation.

1. Ask about Their Plans for the Future

Talk about a future plan, like an occasion that was mentioned during your conversation with them. Ask them if they plan to do anything over the weekend. This implies you should direct the conversation's final topics in the direction you want them to go. They will be open to your closing remarks because discussing their future plans puts them in a positive frame of mind. "Do have a great time with the XYZ plans" is a good note to end the discussion. You will have succeeded in getting them to feel you are concerned about their future plans and to talk about it after the conversation.

2. Propose Meeting up with Them Later

Offer to spend time with them later. When you're talking to a friend or coworker, you can ask if they'd like to go for lunch with you, and if they agree, you've successfully created an avenue to share mutual interests. You can end the conversation by saying, "I'd like to continue this conversation during our lunch." They will happily walk away anticipating lunch and feeling good about your conversation with them.

3. Look Uninterested

If you are the listener and want to end a conversation, look into the distance rather than directly at the speaker. Most speakers expect you to look at them from time to time to demonstrate your interest in what they are saying, and if you look away for too long, they will likely get the message. Sometimes it's hard to express your disinterest in a conversation, and you have to rely on passing an indirect message and hoping the speaker gets the hint.

4. Make a Departure Hint

At the climax of the conversation, as you notice energy dwindling, prepare their minds to expect an end at any moment by saying, "One last thing before I leave." Because you informed them beforehand, they won't have the impression that you are being rude. Even if you carry on talking for a while, they are already aware of your intention to end the conversation sometime soon.

5. Pretend You're Checking in with the Host

If you initiate a conversation with someone at an event, you can use checking in on the host as an exit tactic. If the event is big, you will be seen as popular. Finish your conversation with, "I realize I didn't greet the host. I should leave now. It was a pleasure speaking with you." You can use this on friends or strangers to escape an awkward situation and get some fresh air.

6. Point Your Toes to the Exit

This strategy works if the speaker notices the hint. Your toes pointing toward an exit indicate you want to leave, and hopefully, the speaker picks up on your cue. This strategy has a low impact because not everyone will understand the message you want to convey, and others will ignore it in a bid to continue boring you by continuing to talk.

7. Distance Yourself

Maintain distance from the speaker, but gradually and step by step. The speaker will soon realize you want to be somewhere else and will dismiss you. If they keep talking, keep putting distance between you until it becomes difficult for them to communicate with you. This is a subtle way of saying you want to leave without actually saying so.

8. Finish with a Summary of Their Story

During the conversation, pay attention to the other person's great/awkward/awesome/funny memorable story and recall it when you want to end the conversation. This will rekindle their emotions as you express your gratitude for sharing. Finish the conversation by saying, "I'm so glad we met. I appreciate you sharing this lovely story; I could identify with it. It's been fantastic!" Remembering a story tells them you were paying attention, and they won't feel awkward when you close the conversation.

9. Take Advantage of Your WristWatch

Keep looking at your watch to convey the message that you are in a hurry. A non-verbal signal can easily be ignored by a stubborn speaker, but you can make it clearer by mentioning the time. The conversation could end with something like, "Wow, the time has really flown by, and I never noticed. It's already getting late. It was a pleasure to meet you." You can now walk away without feeling uncomfortable.

10. Set a Time Limit

A subtler version of checking your watch is to inform them you will be leaving in a few minutes. This is similar to setting a time limit for the conversation to keep all parties informed. By saying, "I should go in a few minutes, even though I would have loved to hear more stories," you have told them your time is limited and you need to end the conversation.

11. Excuse Yourself

Saying "Excuse me, please" will end a conversation." You don't have to explain why you need to be excused. You either need to speak to someone else or go somewhere. In any case, excusing yourself has made clear your wish to depart.

12. Take Advantage of Your Family or Friend

Pointing to a friend or acquaintance will also effectively end the conversation. The other person may feel less important or interesting as a result, but you are under no obligation to explain. Say, "Oh, there's my friend. Although I enjoyed our conversation, I must go and see him/her".

13. Send Your Regards to a Mutual Friend

Is your conversation with a friend? If you have mentioned a relative, friend, or acquaintance during your conversation, you can use this to draw a conclusion. Simply tell them to give your regards to the person, saying, "I have to go but don't forget to tell our friend I said hello!"

14. Excuse Them

If you met the person while they were doing something and interrupted them with a conversation, end the conversation by excusing yourself and allowing them to continue their chores. Say something like, "It was great talking with you. I should leave you to finish your chores now."

15. Use Handshake

Surprisingly, handshakes are also used to end conversations. You can start and end a conversation with a handshake, but you must wait for it to be accepted. Consider asking someone for directions and, when they've finished, offer a handshake and thank them. Although it depends on the situation and the individuals involved, this is a professional way to end a conversation.

16. Look around for Inspiration

Look around your surroundings for a cue to help you exit a conversation. It could be the food you're eating reminding you of dinner to be made at home, or it could be an approaching train you must board. You can say, "That's the next train. I shouldn't miss this one to avoid getting home late." Look around you for whatever the cue.

17. Take a Seat or Take a Walk

If you have the conversation standing, ask to be seated as a way to end it. If you've been sitting for a while, you can also ask to stand or go for a walk. The idea is to use the opposite of what you're doing as an excuse to end the conversation. End the conversation with "Wow! We've been standing for a long time. I'll go take a seat now. I thoroughly enjoyed our conversation!" In situations like this, relief is understandable.

18. Use Home as an Exit Strategy

You can use the desire to return home as an exit strategy. Any justification for your hasty return should be relatable and plausible. It could be to assist your partner, to help your parent make a stop at the stores, or to arrive home early before your loved ones become concerned. The conversation is concluded with, "Is it already that late? I need to get going before my parents become concerned!" Don't lie because you may run into your conversation partner again if you don't get home on time.

19. Make a Phone Call

Phone calls can come to your rescue when you need to end a conversation smoothly. You can call a friend, family or colleague. You should conclude your conversation by saying, "I would have loved to continue chatting, but I need to call someone right now. Hope we can talk later?"

20. Exchange Contact Information

Is it a networking event for professionals? Then you should have already exchanged contact information, which you can use to end the conversation, as you say: "It was a pleasure speaking to you. I will send you an email." This generates a lot of hope, expectation, and excitement.

21. Thank Them

"Thank you" is a simple way to end a conversation without ruining the mood. Make direct eye contact while saying it with sincerity. Remember, they can see your emotions through your eyes, so be genuine in your appreciation. Conclude the conversation with "Thank you for chatting; I should be leaving now. Goodbye."

22. Use Gestures at the Workplace

In the workplace, gestures can be used to end conversations rather than actual words. You can walk up to the exit door and hold the handle to signal your wish to leave. Alternatively, walk with the person toward their office or desk rather than offering them a seat in yours. Ask if you can meet them later because you have unfinished business to attend to first. Offer to continue the conversation after lunch, or you can kindly remind them of their unfinished work and send them on their way. In a fast-paced setting like the working world, it's easy to pick up on cues and end conversations without feeling awkward or stressed.

23. Tell Them Your Battery Is Running Low

If you're on a call or video call, you can end it quickly by saying your battery is low, you need to switch to another call, or the connection is bad, so you'll call back later. Tell them you can't talk while driving and promise you'll call back. Always say you will call them back later when you want to end a video or phone call abruptly. Once the call's agenda is finished, say goodbye and thank the other party.

When you end conversations well, you can leave a lasting memory and make amazing friendships no matter where you are or who you are talking to. If your exit strategy complements your chat partner and makes the person feel memorable and liked, you have made a grand exit. One single exit strategy to achieve this during a conversation is "It has been so wonderful speaking to you. I will certainly remember you." This type of conversation ender will warm the heart of anyone who hears it.

How to End a Conversation with a Chatterbox

Even when you're not paying attention, this type of person can talk you to death. It seems they would rather speak and have their opinions heard. Don't give a coworker a chance to get comfortable in their chatter. Remind them you have a task to do and will return to the conversation when you have time. It is easier to end conversations with your coworkers if you use gestures to indicate you are busy or if you position yourself close to the door, ready to leave as soon as you can.

If you meet a stranger and they turn out to be a chatterbox, you can fake a phone call to get them to stop talking while also giving you an opportunity to escape. Look away and rarely respond to their conversation. Hopefully, they'll get the message and end the conversation. It can be difficult to end conversations without appearing rude when you're the listener. When all other methods of signaling the chatterbox have failed, you can use the silent treatment. Keep quiet, and they'll stop talking when you don't respond.

How to End a Conversation When Someone Shows Disinterest

As the speaker, you should be able to notice when your chat partner has lost interest in the conversation. One way is to observe their body language. Signs of boredom will include a loss of focus, eye contact, and distraction, which is a clear sign that it's time to end the conversation.

In situations like this, use some of the following methods to end the conversation without losing any dignity.

- Appreciate them for their time and say goodbye. Keep it simple and straightforward.

- Ask to make use of the restroom. This is also an easy way if you are in a place with a restroom.

- Excuse the person to get back to what they were doing when you met them.

- Quickly make a phone call and excuse yourself. Phone calls have helped many people end conversations, especially boring ones.

- Compliment something about them, maybe their smile or hair, and ask to leave immediately.

Picture yourself enjoying a mouthwatering meal and then getting a terrible dessert. It's not the nice meal, but the awful dessert that will be the first thing you recall. This is comparable to a conversation where the first impression was positive, but the last impression wasn't the same. Poor first impressions can be rescued if you leave a great last impression. If you strike up a conversation, prepare an escape route in advance. Stop talking when people are excited and interested. You'd have a better chance of meeting and speaking to them again if you ended your previous conversation on a positive note.

An all-around exit strategy, regardless of what was discussed or where the conversation is taking place, would be to thank your chat partner for their time and tell them you look forward to seeing them later. You can say things like, "I enjoyed speaking with you. I hope to do it again another time," "It was nice seeing you again, thank you for coming," and "I am grateful our paths crossed."

Conclusion

Improving your communication skills can elevate several aspects of your professional and private life. Effective communication gives us a way to understand events, people, and situations successfully without leaving much room for misinterpretation. Good communicators adapt well to diverse environments and help you get along well with people. They are also able to cultivate mutual respect and trust with everyone around them, as well as create a healthy space for problem-solving and generating innovative ideas.

It is widely believed that employees' productivity can be improved by encouraging good organization-wide communications. Many people think that interacting with others is easy, especially those who have never interacted with someone from a different background or hold significantly different opinions and beliefs. There is always a chance of disconnection in mutual understanding, which could reach the point of boiling anger and conflict. However, working on your communication skills teaches you how to communicate your point of view and process that of others while keeping your head and emotions in check.

Being an excellent communicator will always make you valuable. However, it has become a particularly crucial skill in today's modern age. We consume a large amount of information while talking to people, scrolling through social media, shopping, watching TV, or running errands every single day. Having good communication skills allows us to feel less overwhelmed because it helps us decode the messages being delivered to us. Communication is not just about sharing and sending information. It also has a lot to do with how we receive, process, and react to it, and it enables us to gain insight into the emotions behind the messages we receive.

Strong communication enriches our personal and professional relationships. It makes us better decision-makers and encourages us to compromise in difficult situations. Being able to express ourselves and speak our minds with ease can boost our confidence and make us more assertive.

The best communicators are often the first ones to come up with great solutions. They are advocates and initiators of change, inspiring and motivating those around them. This is why a lack of communication skills can be a deal breaker in the work environment. It can also put relationships on the line.

While some people are talented, eloquent speakers, others require more practice to get their messages through to an audience. While it takes a lot of time and effort, anyone can become an excellent communicator if they put their mind to it. Now that you have read this book, you know how to strike up conversations, actively listen to people, improve your social intelligence, master the art of storytelling and improve your public speaking. This book is the key to improved communication skills and effective interactions. Applying the knowledge provided in this guide can help you avoid misinterpretations and improve all your relationships. The better your communication skills, the higher the levels of mutual trust and respect you will gain in your interactions.

Here's another book by Andy Gardner that you might like

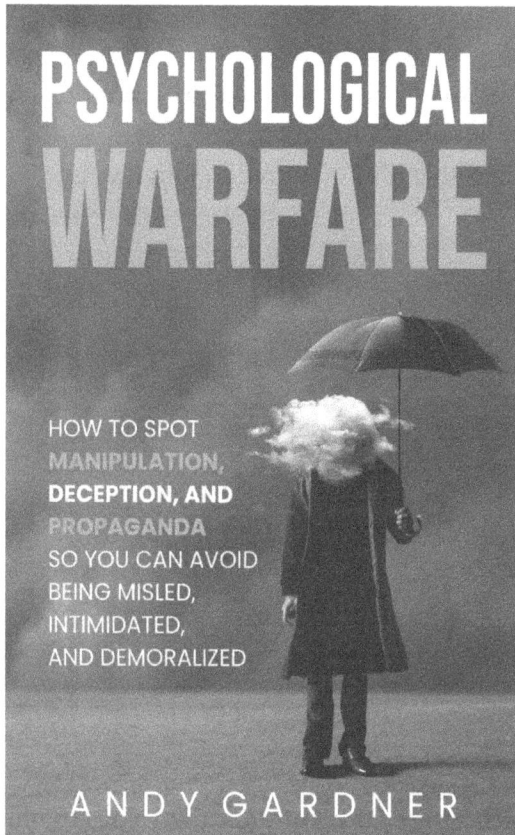

PSYCHOLOGICAL WARFARE

HOW TO SPOT MANIPULATION, DECEPTION, AND PROPAGANDA SO YOU CAN AVOID BEING MISLED, INTIMIDATED, AND DEMORALIZED

ANDY GARDNER

Free Bonus from Andy Gardner

Hi!

My name is Andy Gardner, and first off, I want to THANK YOU for reading my book.

Now you have a chance to join my exclusive email list related to human psychology and self-development so you can get the ebook below for free as well as the potential to get more ebooks for free! Simply click the link below to join.

P.S. Remember that it's 100% free to join the list.

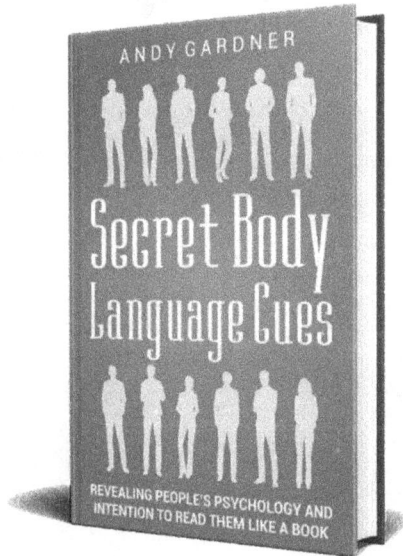

Access your free bonuses here:
https://livetolearn.lpages.co/communication-skills-training-paperback/

References

What are communication skills? Types and importance of communication skillsASM IBMR

7 types of communication skills - verbal, non-verbal. (2022, February 2). CourseMentorTM. https://coursementor.com/blog/types-of-communication-skills/

American English Skills Development Center. (2022, April 5). What are the benefits of effective communication skills. Linkedin.com. https://www.linkedin.com/pulse/what-benefits-effective-communication-/?trk=organization-update-content_share-article

CLIMB Professional Development, & Training. (2019, July 9). The 7 benefits of effective communication in personal and professional settings. Pcc.edu. https://climb.pcc.edu/blog/the-7-benefits-of-effective-communication-in-personal-and-professional-settings

Five types of communication. (2018, July 12). Graduate College of Drexel University. https://drexel.edu/graduatecollege/professional-development/blog/2018/July/Five-types-of-communication/

Caputa, P. (2018, April 23). Active listening in sales: The ultimate guide. HubSpot. https://blog.hubspot.com/sales/active-listening-guide

Ld, C. (2012, May 3). Successful communication is a two way street. Catalyst Learning & Development. https://cbduk.wordpress.com/2012/05/03/successful-communication-is-a-two-way-street/

Saha, S. (n.d.). Active listening: How important this skill is in mentoring? Mentoringcomplete.com

Carpenter, D. (2015, November 25). 3 ways to build real empathy for others in your life. Verywell Mind. https://www.verywellmind.com/how-to-develop-empathy-in-relationships-1717547

Cherry, K. (2006, September 8). What is emotional intelligence? Verywell Mind. https://www.verywellmind.com/what-is-emotional-intelligence-2795423

Cherry, K. (2015, January 5). What is empathy? Verywell Mind. https://www.verywellmind.com/what-is-empathy-2795562

Dial, M. (2019, July 30). Five everyday exercises for building empathy. INSEAD Knowledge. https://knowledge.insead.edu/career/five-everyday-exercises-building-empathy

In Professional Development. (2022, April 1). 3 ways Emotional Intelligence will improve your communication. Inpd.co.uk. https://www.inpd.co.uk/blog/3-ways-emotional-intelligence-will-improve-your-communication?hs_amp=true

Jacobson, S. (2016, May 5). Emotional awareness - what it is and why you need it. Harley TherapyTM Blog; Harley Therapy. https://www.harleytherapy.co.uk/counselling/emotional-awareness.htm

Schmitz, T. (2016, June 3). The importance of emotional awareness in communication. The Conover Company. https://www.conovercompany.com/the-importance-of-emotional-awareness-in-communication/

Turning Point Resolutions Inc. (2021, May 21). 10 tips for improving your nonverbal communication. Turning Point Resolutions Inc. https://turningpointresolutions.com/10-tips-for-improving-your-nonverbal-communication/

Clear, J. (2013, July 25). How to be confident and reduce stress in 2 minutes per day. James Clear. https://jamesclear.com/body-language-how-to-be-confident

Cherry, K. (2017, July 27). Understanding body language and facial expressions. Verywell Mind. https://www.verywellmind.com/understand-body-language-and-facial-expressions-4147228

Spence, J. (2020, February 18). Nonverbal communication: How body language & nonverbal cues are key. Lifesize. https://www.lifesize.com/en/blog/speaking-without-words/

Forbes Coaches Council. (2018, October 18). 11 nonverbal ways to express empathy and camaraderie with your team. Forbes. https://www.forbes.com/sites/forbescoachescouncil/2018/10/18/11-nonverbal-ways-to-express-empathy-and-camaraderie-with-your-team/?sh=7d8033605151

Barnum, C., & Wolniansky, N. (1989, June). Taking cues from body language. Management Review, 78, 59+. https://go.gale.com/ps/i.do?id=GALE%7CA7640467&sid=googleScholar&v=2.1&it=r&linkaccess=abs&issn=00251895&p=AONE&sw=w&userGroupName=anon%7E16cb9f2b

Canada, A. (2019, April 17). Effective Communication - Improving your Social Skills. Anxiety Canada. https://www.anxietycanada.com/articles/effective-communication-improving-your-social-skills/

Waters, S. (n.d.). How to make a good first impression: Expert tips and tricks. Betterup.com. https://www.betterup.com/blog/how-to-make-a-good-first-impression

Young Entrepreneur Council. (2019, April 3). 11 tips for making A great first impression with new clients. Forbes. https://www.forbes.com/sites/theyec/2019/04/03/11-tips-for-making-a-great-first-impression-with-potential-new-clients/?sh=6b0ce195bd4f

How to make a good first impression: 7 tips that really work. (2020, November 25). ZenBusiness Inc. https://www.zenbusiness.com/blog/seven-tips/

Svitorka, T. (2019, July 28). 6 tips How to master small talk and never feel awkward again. Tomas Svitorka - London Life Coach. https://tomassvitorka.com/master-small-talk/

6 tips to master small talk. (2021, February 18). Make Me Better. https://www.makemebetter.net/6-tips-to-master-small-talk/

Viktor Sander B. Sc., B. A., Morin, D. A., & Ashfield, C. (2020, October 22). How to make conversation as an introvert. SocialSelf. https://socialself.com/blog/make-conversation-introvert/

Thorp, T. (2020, March 16). 10 ways to deepen your connections with others. Chopra. https://chopra.com/articles/10-ways-to-deepen-your-connections-with-others

Mokhtar, N. H., Halim, M. F. A., & Kamarulzaman, S. Z. S. (2011). The effectiveness of storytelling in enhancing communicative skills. Procedia, Social and Behavioral Sciences, 18, 163–169. https://doi.org/10.1016/j.sbspro.2011.05.024

Nandy, P. (2017, March 22). 5 ways storytelling can be used to improve communication. Com.au. https://www.insidehr.com.au/how-top-companies-use-storytelling-to-drive-results/

Parekh, D. (2019, October 14). Communicate your Point of View through storytelling. Forbes.

https://www.forbes.com/sites/forbescoachescouncil/2019/10/14/communicate-your-point-of-view-through-storytelling/?sh=54821be541bf

Sundin, A., Andersson, K., & Watt, R. (2018). Rethinking communication: integrating storytelling for increased stakeholder engagement in environmental evidence synthesis. Environmental Evidence, 7(1), 1–6. https://doi.org/10.1186/s13750-018-0116-4

Woodget, M. (2022, February 10). The importance of storytelling. Go Narrative! https://www.gonarrative.com/blog/2022/2/10/the-importance-of-storytelling

Ahmed, A. (2010, July 30). Effective Group Communication Processes. Small Business - Chron.com; Chron.com. https://smallbusiness.chron.com/effective-group-communication-processes-3187.html

Festinger, L., & Thibaut, J. (1951). Interpersonal communication in small groups. Journal of Abnormal Psychology, 46(1), 92–99. https://doi.org/10.1037/h0054899

Gail, C. (n.d.). Team Communication: Effective Group Collaboration & Teamwork. Crystalknows.com. https://www.crystalknows.com/blog/team-communication

Quinn, J. (2020, November 3). How much of communication is nonverbal? The University of Texas Permian Basin | UTPB; The University of Texas Permian Basin. https://online.utpb.edu/about-us/articles/communication/how-much-of-communication-is-nonverbal/

8 fears of public speaking and how to overcome them. (2016, November 17). Elaine Powell website: https://elainepowell.com/all-posts/8-fears-of-public-speaking-and-how-to-overcome-them/

A guide to confidence in public speaking. (2021, April 26). Throughline Group website: https://www.throughlinegroup.com/resources/confidence-in-public-speaking/

Brown, M. (2011, April 18). What Are the Problems of Public Speaking? Pen and the Pad website: https://penandthepad.com/info-8247710-problems-public-speaking.html

Expert Panel®. (2021, July 15). How to fix 14 public speaking issues professionals commonly overlook. Forbes website: https://www.forbes.com/sites/forbescoachescouncil/2021/07/15/how-to-fix-14-public-speaking-issues-professionals-commonly-overlook/?sh=43c8a9b04c14

Genard, G. (n.d.). 10 fast and effective ways to overcome stage fright. Genardmethod.com website: https://www.genardmethod.com/blog/10-fast-and-effective-ways-to-overcome-stage-fright

LaDouceur, P. (n.d.). What we fear more than death. Mentalhelp.net website: https://www.mentalhelp.net/blogs/what-we-fear-more-than-death/

Cooke, E. (2012, January 15). How narratives can aid memory. The Guardian. https://www.theguardian.com/lifeandstyle/2012/jan/15/story-lines-facts

Sheeran, P. (2002). Intention behavior relations: A conceptual and empirical review. European Review of Social Psychology, 12(1), 1–36. https://doi.org/10.1080/14792772143000003

Spence, G. (1996). How to argue and win every time, at home, at work, in court, everywhere, every day. Sidgwick & Jackson.

Splitter, J., & Danielle Murphy, L. (n.d.). How to have healthier arguments. Everydayhealth.com. https://www.everydayhealth.com/emotional-health/how-to-have-healthier-arguments-according-to-psychologists/

Stone, D. (1999). Difficult Conversations: How to Discuss what Matters Most. Michael Joseph.

The link and story methods. (n.d.). Mindtools.com. https://www.mindtools.com/pages/article/newTIM_01.htm

Van Edwards, V. (2020, August 27). 62 ways to politely end a conversation in ANY situation. Science of People. https://www.scienceofpeople.com/end-conversation/

Miller, K. (2021, November 18). 12 tips for how to end a conversation instead of dying a thousand deaths in moments of awkward silence. Well+Good. https://www.wellandgood.com/how-to-end-conversation/

Jones, B. (2017, June 1). How to end a conversation: Strategies and expressions you can use. Get More Vocab; Bradford Jones. https://getmorevocab.com/strategies-expressions-ending-conversation/

Top 5 communication skills and how to improve them. (2022, February 22). Haiilo. https://haiilo.com/blog/top-5-communication-skills-and-how-to-improve-them/